BETTER THINGS ARE YET TO COME

BETTER THINGS ARE YET TO COME

Traveling on the Tides of Life

Alice Champagne

Heavenly
Light Press
Alpharetta, Georgia

The author has tried to recreate events, locations, and conversations from his/her memories of them. In some instances, in order to maintain their anonymity, the author has changed the names of individuals and places. He/she may also have changed some identifying characteristics and details such as physical attributes, occupations, and places of residence.

Copyright © 2024 by Alice Champagne

All rights reserved. No part of this book may be reproduced or transmitted in any form or by any means, electronic or mechanical, including photocopying, recording, or any information storage and retrieval system, without permission in writing from the author.

ISBN: 978-1-6653-0931-8 – Paperback
eISBN: 978-1-6653-0932-5 – eBook

These ISBNs are the property of Heavenly Light Press (a Division of BookLogix) for the express purpose of sales and distribution of this title. The content of this book is the property of the copyright holder only. Heavenly Light Press does not hold any ownership of the content of this book and is not liable in any way for the materials contained within. The views and opinions expressed in this book are the property of the Author/Copyright holder, and do not necessarily reflect those of Heavenly Light Press/BookLogix.

Scripture quotations marked "ESV" are from the ESV® Bible (The Holy Bible, English Standard Version®), copyright © 2001 by Crossway, a publishing ministry of Good News Publishers. Used by permission. All rights reserved.

Scripture quotations marked "NIV" are taken from the Holy Bible, New International Version®, NIV®. Copyright © 1973, 1978, 1984, 2011 by Biblica, Inc.™ Used by permission of Zondervan. All rights reserved worldwide.

Scripture quotations marked "NLT" are taken from the Holy Bible, New Living Translation, copyright © 1996, 2004, 2007 by Tyndale House Foundation. Used by permission of Tyndale House Publishers, Inc., Carol Stream, Illinois 60188. All rights reserved.

Scripture quotations marked "TLB" are from The Living Bible copyright © 1971 by Tyndale House Foundation. Used by permission of Tyndale House Publishers Inc., Carol Stream, Illinois 60188. All rights reserved. The Living Bible, TLB, and the The Living Bible logo are registered trademarks of Tyndale House Publishers.

∞This paper meets the requirements of ANSI/NISO Z39.48-1992 (Permanence of Paper)

Author Photo by Masha Champagne Photography

090924

This book is dedicated to my family.

My prayer for each of you is that you know beyond a shadow of a doubt that I love you! And that God loves you even more! I also wrote this to help those of you who feel abandoned, unloved, alone, or without purpose. I pray that you will see God's fingerprints all over your life. You are uniquely made and loved.

One of my life verses is from Jeremiah 17:7-8 (NLT), which says, "But blessed are those who trust in the Lord and have made the Lord their hope and confidence. They are like trees planted along a riverbank, with roots that reach deep into the water. Such trees are not bothered by the heat or worried by long months of drought. Their leaves stay green, and they never stop producing fruit."

I write about my life to not only help my roots grow deeper, and my hope and confidence in the Lord be stronger, but for you to remember all the fruit He has produced in your life.

I pray that you do not define yourself by looking in the rear-view mirror but by what lies ahead of you. As you read my story, I hope with all my heart that my stones of remembrance help you recognize all the blessings in your own life because better things are yet to come.

CONTENTS

Introduction
ix

The Living Water
1

A Nautical Journey
11

Across Two Oceans
15

Ebb and Flow
21

Storms and Crashing Waves
41

Coming Ashore
47

Moana
65

Faithful in the Current
85

Freedom from the Rip Tide
101

A Letter to My Heavenly Father
105

A Letter to My Earthly Father
107

Navigating the Waters of Life
109

Acknowledgments and the Next Thing to Come
111

INTRODUCTION

As my friend Trudy told me, "We all have a story inside of us."

This is my story from my perspective. But more importantly, this is the story of what God did. And what He continues to do.

It's because of Him that I am writing this at all.

I never thought I, Alice, would ever, ever write a book. I don't enjoy writing, and I certainly don't think I am any good at it.

But this is not an ordinary "book." This is my remembrance of what God has done in my life. Not me. As I ponder and marvel at all I have done, I wonder—*how*? I immediately realized it wasn't by my own power but by God walking with me. My choice to trust and have faith in God's unique purpose for me was not always (and still isn't) easy.

It has been like tiny seeds. Tiny seeds God planted in my heart. His watering, tending, pruning, and, yes, taking out old soil and adding new, fresh, life-breathing soil.

And I am about to tell you *how* He did it.

God is calling each of us to memorialize what God has done for us.

Why am I writing this book? Because this book is my "stones of remembrance" to proclaim His great works to others.

> "And they have defeated him by the blood of the Lamb and by their testimony."
>
> —Revelations 12:11 (NLT)

Have you ever been swimming in the ocean and got caught in a rip current? A rip current is a powerful channel of water that flows away from the shore and can be very hazardous to swimmers. Swimming in a rip current can make you feel helpless and very afraid. The strong current pulls you away from the shore and can make even the strongest swimmers powerless. The ebbs and flows of my life have been like the rip current, pulling me out, trying to pull me under. But through it all, my strength, perseverance, and, more importantly, through the will of God, I have *overcome*. This is my story to share, and it's not over yet.

THE LIVING WATER

The truth is that God planted this seed in my heart to write down this memoir, or my story, in 2018. I know that my testimony is supposed to be shared. When we share our story, we help others, specifically the next generation, with our wisdom and the things we have learned, such as important things about our families, where we came from, who our relatives are, and who we are.

I wasn't sure I could share. I had a lot of pain from wounds deep in my heart. Some had *big* scabs that I was not willing to rip off yet. Deep wounds. Even some I didn't yet understand.

I didn't want to tell my story, but I kept feeling a nudging and prompting from the Holy Spirit. I kept finding reasons not to write.

I don't like writing.

I don't have time.

I don't believe anyone wants to read about my life.

I do not want to remember the painful things of the past.

These are my excuses. It is often easier to use excuses to not think about the past because it is painful. Over the years, I have been slowly picking at the scabs and the truth is, it is therapeutic to look not at the wounds but at the scars.

There were a few pivotal reasons why I was finally able to begin writing this book. To be able to recall memories of my past, I first needed to sit with myself and be willing to think about my childhood—something I had always shied away from. I had not, until the start of this, wanted to try. I was stuck.

Ultimately, a series of events was orchestrated (by God) that set me on the path to uncover this narrative. I first read my friend Renee Bradford's book, *Nothing Wasted*. Second, my granddaughter Lilly asked me, "Nana, what was your life like growing up in Hawaii?"

The third event happened during a girls' weekend with one of my "sisters of the heart," Lisa. Off we went to North Carolina for our girls' weekend, where a big breakthrough happened. We discussed a lot of things, as we always do. I mentioned to her I was creating a timeline of my childhood and wanted to bring up memories. This idea was sparked by that book and my granddaughter's question. She, of course, was very supportive.

She booked us a relaxing meditation session at a place called Sound of a New Dawn, which is a sound relaxation therapy based on frequencies that allow your brain to reset or rest. We had a wonderful time, relaxed, and went away feeling refreshed. As we were leaving, we bought mala beads, with their amazing colors and brightness, that spoke to us. We planned to wear them as a necklace or a bracelet. It was also our Mother's Day gift to ourselves. We read each of the cards attached.

My statement read, "The past is my power now, not my weakness."

"Wow," I said. "How coincidental that we were just talking about my past."

This statement not only empowered me but gave me more

confidence that I *am* worthy of talking about my past, and it doesn't have any "bad" power over me anymore. I felt a sense of peace and strength and a belief that I would be okay. I would be able to recall painful memories as part of my story because it is my power. In other words, this is how God made me and who I am. I am not weak but stronger because of how I grew up. The past is my power now, not my weakness. I am okay. This was the wake-up that I needed to dig deep to get more healing and share it because we are called to.

The fourth prompt was another book called *The Stories We Tell* by Joanna Gaines, which gave me more courage and understanding that I am worthy to share, and my story could help someone else like me. Go figure. Hear me laughing, realizing God knows what He is doing if I just listen the first time.

Another big or pivotal reason was number five—a trip to Morocco, Africa, where I was born—but more on this in a later chapter.

And lastly, a photo album of my childhood that my mother made for me and gave to me in 2005. Sadly, I was too angry to appreciate the album fully until I decided to write this story.

Why? I needed more healing. When we dig out the stinky, yucky gunk in our hearts and replace it with gentleness, joy, peace, and, yes, love from God, there is room for God to work. When we rip the band-aid off and allow the scab to heal, we get more healing.

But in doing so, I realized that maybe, just maybe, my words, my stones of remembrance, could help even one person and possibly my family.

Because of the hurt that I was carrying around, my children did not know much about my childhood. I didn't talk about it, and since my parents were divorced, there was no childhood home or grandparents to visit. As my children grew, they saw *my* pain, and therefore, I held back talking about my childhood or memories. They even had some hurts of their own from their/our relationship with my mother (their Granny). Today, as I think about my children and their children, I am sad that the relationship with "Granny," Marjorie Harper, was not stronger. And for that matter, relationships with other extended family as well.

As my children became young adults and their grandmother, aged, it became more difficult to have a healthy relationship with her due to how she treated me and my family. As a result, I was forced over the years to set boundaries to limit my feelings of being inadequate, seeking validation from others, and being critical of myself.

Then, my children had children. Sadly, my grandchildren never knew their great-grandmother, although there could have been opportunities. Throughout all these years, I continued to go to therapy, at one point even going to Families Anonymous and Celebrate Recovery (Twelve-step programs). Healing is hard work!!!!

I'm so thankful for the healing I have received (I worked hard to get). It's been my hurts that I needed to work through so that I could get to this point and be free of my past. Move forward!

I want my children and their children's children and families to be proud of their family history despite my brokenness from divorce and the physical and emotional separation I felt growing up.

I want my grandchildren to know *all* the good parts of me and, therefore, them, too.

So, like the ocean, deep and wide, clear and blue, I dove in.

I began to believe and accept what God says about me:

> [1] "Do not fear, for I have redeemed you;
> I have summoned you by name; you are mine.
> [2] When you pass through the waters,
> I will be with you;
> and when you pass through the rivers,
> they will not sweep over you.
> When you walk through the fire,
> you will not be burned;
> the flames will not set you ablaze.
> [3] For I am the Lord your God,
> the Holy One of Israel, your Savior."
>
> —Isaiah 43:1-3 (NIV)

God calls me His child. He says I am worthy, loved, and valuable.

Growing up as a middle child, I was constantly trying to keep the peace. I did not like disagreements, anger, or conflict, and I still do not like it to this day. Probably never will, but I have learned how to acknowledge and cope with these feelings somewhat better as an adult. As a child, I did not learn how to express myself. As I grew up, I handled difficulties with an attitude of "just power through," ignoring and burying my true feelings. I was like Dory in the movie *Finding Nemo*, "Just keep swimming!"

I did not feel loved growing up, especially from thirteen years of age on. That was hard to admit. I lacked confidence in myself (I still do, but not nearly as often), and I did not believe people wanted to hear what I had to say.

I felt God wooing me and drawing me to Him after I married Dennis. I felt similarly a few times in college, too, but ignored it mostly. After having children, we wanted to attend church regularly. We felt it was the right thing to do. As a mother, I wanted my children to grow up with a love and belief in God.

But first, I wanted to learn how to be confident in who I was and understand my identity in Christ. You see, the world has a way of getting in your head and making you believe that you are not enough. We have "glasses" we see through, based on our experiences, to help us navigate through life. The glasses also give us the lens of how we feel loved and are typically based on our earthly father figure. Not having strong trust, love, protection and Godly example from my father, I didn't know my heavenly Father. Little did I know in 1986, after joining Christ the King Lutheran Church in Florissant, Missouri, that I would begin a process (and it is a lifelong process) and journey with Jesus holding my hand and walking with me.

Here is a scripture that was a handhold: Proverbs 3:5 (NLT) "Trust in the Lord with all your heart; do not depend on your own understanding." Okay, I get this. That's a baby step since I don't understand why my family is broken.

And another, Ephesians 1:5 (NLT), "God decided in advance to adopt us into his own family by bringing us to himself through Jesus Christ. This is what he wanted to do, and it gave him great pleasure."

I have been adopted as God's child. Okay! I need a father and a family.

One more piece of freedom from Ephesians 2:10 (NLT), "For we are God's masterpiece. He has created us anew in Christ Jesus, so we can do the good things he planned for us long ago."

I looked around to my earthly friends and family. I didn't feel significant to anyone, but I am significant to God. I really needed to believe this deep in my being.

God was very near, and He held me tightly for those years in Florissant when Dennis and I first got married. I wanted to follow Jesus and started to believe, embrace, and be free from what I perceived about myself as unlovable, alone, and unworthy.

The freedom in Christ that I knew of in my brain became a seed in my heart that, little by little, began to grow. Its roots grew in my heart, day by day, year by year, and are firmly rooted in Jesus saying to me, "I am accepted, secure, and significant to God, my Father."

I had not felt this way as a daughter of my biological father. I didn't learn these beliefs as a child or teen. But I'm thankful that God kept pursuing me and that I am able to more fully grasp God's truths about who I am.

Back to figuring out how to get started writing a book about my life. The art of writing a life of remembrance takes *remembering*, right? Taking the pieces and, like a puzzle, piecing them slowly and consistently back together. To begin, I needed to ask myself a few really hard questions.

- Who was the little girl, Alice, who moved around as a "Navy Brat?"
- What formed me to make me who I am today?
- At what point in my life did I decide that I wanted to "be" something? To have a career? Accomplishments?
- When did I decide to have the determination that I would not miss *one* thing that God placed me on this earth to do to fulfill my earthly purpose for His Glory?
- What can I remember about my childhood that my grandchildren would want to know about their Nana?

Yet, for me, to think about memories meant digging deep down in my heart to the little girl who felt abandoned, unloved, and out of place with no home to return to.

One day, I was having coffee with one of my girlfriends,

and I was telling her about my wanting to take some intentional time to reflect and try to write down some of the stories or events in my life.

Just so you know, I have tried to do this before without success. When I turned fifty, I decided that I wanted to be more sensitive to God's calling on my life. Getting in touch with a lot of my feelings, digging deeper, and then writing—this does not come easy for me—I'm an engineer by schooling—I like to analyze and overthink things—so this kind of thinking *really* is hard for me, not to mention the actual writing down of stuff.

My friend said, "Just pray and ask God to bring to mind these milestones or stakes in the ground that may have been life-changing or points of remembrance to you."

The next day—God has a way of guiding me when I listen—I read a devotion, and I want to share part of it with you.

It is a story from the Bible about what God did and how we are supposed to share what God has done in our lives. This story is imprinted on my heart and is a reminder every time I have doubts about whether I should write about myself.

God told us to tell others.

The story tells about when God was using Joshua to lead all the people of Israel across the Jordan River. You may or may not be familiar with the story. You may or may not even believe that God did this. But I do believe that God can and will do far more than what we can ask or imagine. When we acknowledge Him as the miracle worker, we give Him the Glory.

Back to the story, when God did that thing—stopped the flow of the river and held back the water!! And all the people crossed safely.

At the beginning of Joshua Chapter 4 (TLB), *"When all the people were safely across, the Lord said to Joshua,* [2-3] *"Tell the twelve* men chosen for a special task, one from each tribe, each to take a stone from where the priests are standing in the middle of the Jordan, and to carry them out and pile them up as a monument at the place where you camp tonight." ⁴ So Joshua summoned the twelve men ⁵ and told them, "Go out into the middle of the Jordan where the Ark is. Each of you is to carry out a stone on your shoulder—twelve stones in all, one for each of the twelve tribes. ⁶ We will use them to build a monument so that in the future, when your children ask, '**What are these stones for?**' ⁷ you can tell them, 'It is to remind us that the Jordan River stopped flowing when the Ark of God went across!' The monument will be a permanent reminder to the people of Israel of this amazing miracle."

Wow! This really impacted me—God is pleased when we memorialize His good works toward us!

Stones of remembrance and witness. Based on this story, I am using my rocks, my remembrances, to tell others how good God has been to me. To be a light on a hill, to shine in the midst of darkness and hopelessness, which are widespread in our world today.

Therefore, this book is a summary of *my* stones of remembrances and witness to what God has done in my life.

I hope that my story will inspire you to remember and share *your* story.

> ¹³ "Jesus replied, 'Anyone who drinks this water will soon become thirsty again. ¹⁴ But those who drink the water I give will never be thirsty again. It becomes a fresh, bubbling spring within them, giving them eternal life.'"
>
> —John 4:13-14 (NLT)

A NAUTICAL JOURNEY

"Promise me you'll always remember:
You're braver than you believe,
and stronger than you seem,
and smarter than you think!"
—Christopher Robin
Winnie the Pooh

Let me set the scene for all the many adventures and ups and downs I will share with you throughout my story.

My dad was a member of the US Navy. That being said, as a military kid, I lived all the challenges of military life. Affectionately called "Navy brat" meant that we were not just part of military life; when we referred to ourselves as such, we were claiming it! I didn't sign up to move around, but I sure learned a lot! For example, how to pack a box to move. And how to pack a suitcase to travel. Did you know to always pack a swimsuit? You never know when you may be able to swim. It's hard to always feel like the new kid, so I learned how to "blend in." Also, there is a big difference between moving and traveling. We did both. Sometimes, we moved, and this meant packing up everything we owned.

Sometimes, we traveled, and this meant packing a bag to go by car and see things.

I experienced deployments, long separations from my dad, lots of moves, living in other countries, and saying "see ya later" to so many friends. As a kid, I didn't understand most of what was happening every time we moved. I was told, "We are moving," and thought, "Here we go again. Pack up and get ready for the next adventure." The truth is, I didn't necessarily believe it was an "adventure." However, my parents did their best to ease the consequences of moving every three to four years. In my young mind, having an adventure attitude equated to a "make the best of the situation" mindset, which would constitute, in my later years, denial, coping with my feelings, and what professionals call survival. Sure, I had feelings of excitement, but sadness too.

I moved houses, I changed schools, and I had no choice but to adapt to new neighborhoods and, of course, new friends. This constantly changing lifestyle can be hard and beneficial but lends itself to making military kids resilient, adaptable, and adventurous.

It can also be isolating, lonely, and depressing.

I learned to accept change and adapt to difficulties.

I tried to find my inner courage after being the new kid or a foreigner in a strange land. This was my hardest task since I was very shy by nature. My nickname from my mother was "shrinking violet," the flower that tries to hide.

Yet, I am now proud to say that the military lifestyle and its experiences forced me to grow into a confident, curious, and courageous woman.

It certainly was not easy, and I wasn't given a choice. It took a lot of intention to be brave and adjust but I did it! Military kids are like dandelions. That's the symbol for a

Navy kid. Why? We are like weeds; we can grow anywhere. My roots may be deep and strong now, but life can be traumatic for a kid moving every few years. One positive that came out of being a military kid is I like to try new things. I like change. I bloom where I am planted. No matter the environment, I prosper and thrive!

I also cherish the song from my scouting days, "Make New Friends" from the Girl Scout songbook, and this verse in particular, "Make new friends but keep the old. One is silver, the other is gold." A friend was like gold to me.

Did you know that military kids say goodbye more often in their first few years than the average person does in a lifetime?

Moving was just part of life—that's what I knew. Probably the best result of being a military kid is that I love to see the world and experience new things!

Thankfully, I married a man who also grew up traveling for vacations and enjoys visiting other places and cities. Of course, he didn't move around or travel as much as I did, but he enjoys it, too, and it's wonderful to have that in common.

Here are all the places I lived as a military kid and after:

- 1960–1961 Kenitra, Morocco, Africa
- 1961–1963 Suitland, Maryland
- 1963–1965 Norfolk, Virginia
- 1965–1968 Wahiawa, Oahu, Hawaii
- 1968–1971 Pensacola, Florida
- 1972–1977 Pearl City, Oahu, Hawaii
- 1977–1978 Marianas Island, Guam, US Territory

- Jan 1979–May 1984 Carbondale, Illinois — Southern Illinois University
- May 1984 Graduated from College
- June 23, 1984 Married Dennis James Champagne
- 1984–1991 Florissant, Missouri
- 1991 Current Marietta, Georgia

Often, our family lived in naval housing or "on base." Sometimes we rented a house. On the last or second tour in Hawaii, we bought a house in Pacific Palisades, Pearl City, Oahu, because my parents were planning to retire and call Hawaii a permanent home.

Before I was five years old, I had traveled across both the Atlantic and the Pacific Oceans on US Naval ships!

ACROSS TWO OCEANS

As a child, I always got nervous when I was asked, "Where are you from?"

Does "where are you from" mean where you were born? Or does "where are you from" mean where you lived the longest from birth to eighteen years of age or adulthood? My answer would change as often as the sun rose and set each day.

I was embarrassed to say I was from Morocco, primarily due to the questions that would come after. A common response from my young peers would be, "Where is that?" or "Why?" I would say, "Africa. My father was in the Navy; that's why he was stationed there." I would get weird looks—scrunched-up faces, thinking, huh? One time, one kid even asked me why I wasn't Black! I didn't know what to say because I thought that was strange. Didn't they know about genetics?

The US Naval Air Station, where my father was stationed, was in the town formerly known as Port Lyautey. The name changed to Kenitra in 1956 and is located about 3.1 miles north-northwest of Kenitra and about ninety miles northeast of Casablanca. The Naval Air Station was turned over to the Royal Moroccan Air Force, and the last of the US military personnel departed the base in 1977.

I was born at the United States Naval Air Station Hospital on October 14, 1960.

Most birth records are one document, maybe two, including one from the hospital with a cute footprint. My birth papers include a Certification of Birth and a form notarized by the Department of State, Foreign Service of the United States of America, REPORT OF A BIRTH ABROAD of a Citizen of the United States of America.

My parents were required to go to the American Embassy in Rabat to report my birth and get the proper documentation and birth certificate, which wasn't officially reported until March 24, 1961. Oh, the intricacies of documenting how someone begins their life when born as a citizen of the United States of America born abroad. My parents were required to show their passports and US Naval ID cards for my report of birth.

My mother always told me that she hoped one day I would go and see where I was born. Sixty-two years later, in 2023, I visited Kenitra and Rabat, Morocco.

I saw the area where the hospital was located, where I was born, and where I lived for a few months, including the US Naval Air Station, which now holds the Royal Moroccan Air Force and even the beach where my mom and dad went with my brother (she was pregnant with me). While I do not remember living there for those first seven months of my life, I am grateful for the pictures on the Moroccan beach.

1960 — Rabat, Morocco, Africa
Mother (Marjorie), pregnant with Alice Jeanne, enjoying the Moroccan beach with father (Charles) and brother Charles Jr. (age twenty-one months).

2023 — Rabat, Morocco, Africa
Alice, sixty-three years later, experiencing her Moroccan birthplace!

I embraced every second of the short three-day visit. After landing in Casablanca, we settled in our hotel and made a short walk to enjoy an authentic Moroccan dinner. We were anxiously waiting for our driver, Mohammed, who met us the following morning. Little were we aware of a law that prohibited him from being a "guide" as well as our driver, so his not speaking English was a significant challenge. Yet, we were with him for the next two days, and, as people do, we found ways to communicate with each other, pointing, grunting, and making gestures, and our mutual word gists got through to each other.

Mohammed took us to Rabat, the country's capital, on the outskirts of Kenitra, and then up to a mountain town called Chefchaouen, more commonly referred to as the "Blue City," where we stayed the night in a Riad, which is a family home hotel.

The next morning, we met our "Guide," Asalashalom, who *did* speak English. He asked me why we were visiting Morocco. What brought us here? Smiling, I told him, "I'm here to see where I was born. You have met an American Moroccan." He said, "No, a Moroccan." He shook my hand as we smiled at each other.

We spoke to him about our Kenitra trip portion and how we had three other places we needed to see on our return drive later that day. He spoke to Mohammed, and all was well. We had to pay a little extra, but it was worth it because, well, that was the reason we were there in the first place. To see the area where I was born.

After an early morning stroll (keeping up with the quick walking eighty-two-year-old guide was not easy) through the lovely "Blue City," we were prepared to head back to Kenitra to explore.

I had brought with me a list of places I needed to see and wanted to make sure I closed the loop on being able to make this dream come true by seeing and experiencing my birth country.

How did I feel as I traveled throughout the country where I was born? Even though I only spent three days on Moroccan soil, I felt complete to be in the very land, to touch the earth I had barely touched as a child—a "this is where it all started" connection. I felt fulfilled and happy. It was a connection to something deep within me—a root grounded in the soil of my heart.

Most importantly, I felt my mother's presence and sensed peace. I heard her say, "You did it! You made it to see where you were born!" It felt like a breath of fresh air, completing a circle that I needed more than I could ask for or imagine.

> "Let the Beloved of the Lord rest secure in Him, for He shields him all day long, and the one the Lord loves rests between His shoulders."
>
> —Deuteronomy 33:12 (NIV)

EBB AND FLOW

GRANDPARENTS AND GREAT-GRANDPARENTS

In 1961, my parents, brother, and I, only seven months old, flew from Morocco to Cadiz, Spain, where we boarded a US Naval ship to sail across the Atlantic to New York City. Can you imagine sailing across the Atlantic Ocean as a baby? I remember my mom explaining to me that since I was allergic to milk at the time, the ship had a short delay in departing due to the need to find an alternative, soy milk, for me to have during the voyage. While I do not remember the trip, I can only imagine what it was like for me and my family on the nine-day trip, Was the ocean choppy or calm? Did I see any sea creatures like whales or dolphins, or was it stormy? Was the boat comfortable? Probably not. It was a Navy vessel, not a Royal Caribbean cruise ship. Whatever the sailing conditions were, I can visualize the ocean as deep and vast.

From there, we went to Billings, Montana. Why Montana? My parents were "from" Billings. Both sets of my grandparents or their parents lived there. Both families were military families and had settled or retired from the military in Montana when my parents were in their teens. My parents met in high school. They were very young when they got married. My father joined the Navy when he was almost eighteen, and my mom was seventeen.

It was during this visit with Nana and Grandpa in Billings, Montana, that I was baptized as a baby in 1961. They were proud Lutherans, and my parents were expected to attend their Lutheran Church. I don't think my mother and father were particularly religious, but it was very important to Nana and Grandpa that we were baptized in the church.

In the years that followed, we moved around a lot, so we never lived near any family. Ever. This especially bothered me in my later years when I met other families, and *all* the relatives lived in the *same* city.

But for us, it was always an ebb and flow—visit and leave. Travel in a car, visit then pack it up.

I do remember my mother talking a lot about her parents and her grandparents and my dad's parents and grandparents. We didn't see them often enough for me to get to know my grandparents well on my own, so this was her way of making sure we "knew" who they were. And I loved learning about them and visiting them.

My Grandparents on my father's side were the Martratts.

Charles Omar Martratt married Virginia Alice Rendo, and they had two children, my father (Charles Austin Martratt) and his sister, ten years younger, (Sherrie Lyn) my Auntie Sherrie. They lived in Albany, New York, and then Billings, Montana, for over thirty years, and finally, Oak Harbor, on Whidbey Island, Washington. My grandfather Martratt and his brother, my Uncle Bob, succeeded in documenting the Martratt ancestry.

I called my Grandparents on my father's side, Nana and Grandpa. This Grandpa gave me away at my wedding since my father was (and still is) in Guam, but more on that later. Since we moved around a lot and didn't see them often, Nana would send me birthday cards forwarded to wherever our military place of duty was at the time. We would speak to them on the phone sometimes, too. I have fond memories of visiting them when we were traveling to our next duty station. I have good memories of them in my life so it is no surprise that after I married Dennis, they visited us a few times when our kids were young. Once a month, Grandpa would call me, with Nana on their second landline (before smart phones kids!) phone in another room, asking me and Dennis how we were doing. We also visited them on one of our national park vacations.

In 2009, my son John and I went to Oak Harbor to celebrate their sixty-fifth wedding anniversary. Despite living away from my grandparents for my entire life, I felt they wanted to know me, and I appreciate my mother helping me to understand these roots.

My mother's parents and grandparents were also introduced to me and my mom tried to help me learn about them, too. Her mom, I called Mimi (her name was Eulita Katherine Casey), and I called her dad (his name was William Henry Harper) Grandpa.

Her father, Grandpa Harper, grew up in Arkansas. In fact, my mom was born in Little Rock, Arkansas. She was very close to her grandparents, Leslie Casey and Clara Lentz. I know my mother loved them a lot as she talked about them and her memories of their times together as she was growing up.

But her father didn't like the South, so eventually, he moved the family to Montana when he retired from the US Army as an ophthalmologist, MD and opened his own clinic. My mom, the oldest of six and being a military family too, moved quite a bit. She even lived in Japan and Germany for a while.

Her mother, who was an alcoholic, died at age fifty. I was ten years old, and my mom was only thirty. I don't think it was pleasant or easy growing up in an alcoholic family, especially since she had to help raise her five younger siblings. I think growing up in the 1950s, you didn't realize not talking about things was a cause for emotional issues. Before Mimi passed, she taught my mother a lot of things, which she passed down to me. As hard as it was for my mom, she did her best to teach us and provide us with opportunities to learn new skills. Looking back now, I realize how hard she tried to keep the connection to our extended family even while moving around a lot.

Being an ophthalmologist, Grandpa Harper was the doctor who first identified the coloboma in my left eye at the age of twelve. A coloboma is an eye condition that people are born with. It happens when part of the tissue that makes up the eye is missing when the eye is developing. Fortunately, my coloboma does not affect my vision at all!

ON OUR WAY TO MARYLAND 1961–1963

Before our next Naval station assignment and destination, we traveled by car to visit my great-grandparents, my mom's grandparents (Leslie Jason Casey and Clara Rosetta Lentz), in Little Rock, Arkansas. Visiting was just that in those days. Sit around and talk. Since I was so young, I don't remember my great-grandparents, but I do have a few pics and memories from my mother talking about our visits.

In the early years of my life, my parents didn't have a lot of money. Housing was very expensive, so we lived in a basement apartment when we first moved to Maryland in

1961. My father was stationed at Cheltenham, Maryland, US Naval Communications Systems.

In the summer of 1962, we moved to a nicer apartment in Suitland, Maryland, with a pool and playground. Our mother encouraged us to play outside, and since I enjoyed being outside so much, I was very happy.

I loved playing with dolls, playing in the pool, outside at the playground, and with my older brother, Charles. He was two years older than me, so I stuck to him like bees on honey. I loved my Bubba. I learned how to ride a trike when I was two. I loved dresses and my mother was a great seamstress and sewed many of my clothes.

My younger sister, Melinda, was born in Maryland.

Growing up, we didn't have cell phones like we do today, so most pictures were taken with the old cameras and real film that you then took to a local store to get developed, which took about a week. The pictures I have are of holidays like Easter, Thanksgiving, and Christmas. My mother dressed me up nicely, a special handmade dress, for the pictures and church. In addition to these, I have pictures of most of my birthdays. Birthdays were a time to celebrate ME! And I still love birthdays.

NORFOLK, VIRGINIA, HERE WE COME 1963–1965

After two years stationed in Maryland, my dad got orders to go to Norfolk, Virginia. He was assigned to the USS *Georgetown* ship, working in communications, and was out to sea for months at a time.

The USS *Georgetown* (AGTR-2/AG-165) was a technical research ship acquired by the US Navy to provide a seaborne platform for global eavesdropping on behalf of the National Security Agency. Her designation as a "technical research" ship was her cover story. Equipped with the latest listening devices, a vast array of electronic gear, and a crew of 250 — most of whom held security clearances that allowed them to work in the spy ship's nerve center. This ship was a research vessel and, during the time my dad was on this ship, according to my research, did reconnaissance (eavesdropping and sending info back to Maryland) around Cuba and the Caribbean and off the coast of South America.

Since he was gone so much, I have no memories of my father during this time, and he is not present in the few pictures of me at this age.

I guess I was a typical young child during the two years in Norfolk.

My brother started kindergarten while in Norfolk, so my sister and I watched TV. My favorite shows were Mr. Ed and Captain Kangaroo. In fact, one of my earliest memories was when I was three years old of a toy puppet called Mr. Ed, based on this early 1960s TV show. Mr. Ed was a *talking* horse in black and white. (You can find it on YouTube.) The puppet toy had a string that, when you pulled it, the puppet talked just like Mr. Ed. I was afraid to put my hand in the puppet because I thought it would bite me. Haha! But I did love that talking horse.

My sister and I loved to play on our swing set and ride in our wagon (we would pull each other around). We made up games all the time. One of our favorite games was called "hang heads." Since we shared a room and both of us had twin beds, we would hang our heads off the side, make faces, and talk to each other. We thought this was hilarious and often got us in trouble because we were supposed to be sleeping.

1963—Norfolk, Virginia
Alice and sister, Melinda, riding in their wagon.

1963
More sister fun!

Since my father was often out to sea for months at a time, my mother took us in the summer of 1964 to visit her parents in Billings, Montana. During this visit to Billings, we went to stay at Grandpa Harper's cabin in Nye, Montana. This was the summer my grandfather drove off the road, crashed into the Stillwater River, and flipped the Jeep with my brother and I in the car with him. My brother broke his wrist, and above my eye was cut, but we were generally all okay. Just shocked and scared. Yikes! Melinda wasn't in the Jeep with us. Growing up, us kids would talk about memories, and this was one of them!

BEACH AND HULA GIRL
(HAWAII BOUND 1965-1968)

In the summer of 1965, Dad received orders to be stationed in Honolulu, Hawaii. We set off on a month-long trip from Virginia across the country, first driving to New York, then to Montana, and then to California. We went to the 1964–1965 World's Fair in New York City and visited my great-grandmother Alice Cleary (Nana Martratt's mom; I called her C. C.) in Albany, New York.

Traveling, visiting relatives, and sightseeing in general seem to have always been part of my life. Driving across the States, especially during the summer when I was four years old, was a very eventful trip. As a military kid (often moving), I learned to appreciate 'going places,' so today, I get excited when our family plans a road trip.

After doing some sightseeing in San Francisco, we set sail on the US Naval ship *Barrett* in the summer of 1965 for Honolulu, Hawaii—a trip that took five days. Since it was a military vessel, we arrived and docked in the Navy area of Pearl Harbor!

Do you believe that by the summer before I turned five, I had crossed both the Atlantic and Pacific oceans by ship?

Just as we were starting our new life in Hawaii, I turned five that October in 1965. We lived in Manana, which was Navy housing. I started school, kindergarten, and my brother and I walked to our nearby elementary school.

A treasured memory of mine was being taught and learning the Hawaiian dance hula by taking lessons from Emma Kaheleilani Bishop, also known as "Mama" Bishop. She was a well-known Kumu Hula (hula teacher) as well as a songwriter and singer of ancient Hawaiian music. I didn't need to go to a building or classroom because the Hawaiian dance form called hula can be taught anywhere. Mama Bishop's hula studio or halau hula school was right in our neighborhood, under a covered carport, just down the street from our house. I would walk to the house by the big tree that helped provide shade, join other girls my age (I was six when I began my hula lessons), and learn ancient dance steps. We were also taught some Hawaiian words since the art of hula is the storytelling of cultural memories, places, and people.

It was serious, these hula lessons. Mama was stern but praised me when I correctly danced the ancient steps. I carried my straw bag filled with my own feather rattles, 'ulī'ulī, and other historic dance implements. I learned how to use my 'ili'ili, small smooth river rocks used in your hands like castanets; my ipu, a one-hand gourd tapped with the other hand, and the pu 'Ili, my split bamboo sticks.

I especially treasured the traditional 'ku'u po'o' or grass skirt I wore to dance, including a yellow top (my mother sewed for me), a lei, and the *real* plumeria flower I wore in my hair that we picked in the front yard of our house!

1967—Pearl City, Oahu
Alice ready for her hula lesson with Mama Bishop.

As a seven-year-old, I was a pretty good dancer and *loved* the hula. The Hawaiian name "Maile" was given to me by Mama Bishop, which is a sweet-smelling Hawaiian vine often used to make garland.

When we were young, my mother was a stay-at-home mom and took care of us three kids. I remember having fun playing outside and riding bikes. My dad worked a lot, but the one thing we did a lot together as a family was go to the beach. We went to the beach a lot!! I *loved* the beach. I can now say that the ocean is in my blood and bones. I felt free jumping in the waves. Letting the waves crash over me as I dunked down, I could feel, hear, and sometimes see the churning seawater. I loved the taste of salt water. I loved the feel of the salt drying on my skin when I lay in the sun those times I needed to rest after playing all day.

1967—Waianae Beach, Oahu
Wave jumping!

We built sandcastles. We buried each other in the sand and then played like we were monsters and chased each other into the sea. My brother would get seaweed and chase me down the beach, trying to "touch" me with the yucky stuff. Ugh. I didn't like the feel of seaweed in or out of the water/ocean. Honestly, I was kind of scared of the seaweed. I hunted for shells but didn't start collecting shells until I was much older. We probably couldn't take them when we moved all the time.

Hawaii was fabulous. I loved the ocean!! I loved swimming. I loved the sand. I loved everything about living on a tropical island. More importantly, I hated leaving it!

1968-1972 BACK TO THE MAINLAND

My dad was transferred again back to the mainland to Pensacola, Florida, which has a large Naval station. This is where I began my Girl Scout adventures. I tried out cheerleading and was on the "prancing team" for my brother's football team.

We got our first and only dog, Butch. He was a beagle, German shepherd mutt. We took Butch with us to Hawaii (again), Guam, and then back to the mainland again (Billings, Montana) in 1978, where he eventually passed away. We loved that dog.

THE ANCHOR OF SCOUTING

Scouting provided the security I needed as we continued to be transferred by the Navy from place to place. Like an anchor, usually a heavy device, normally made of metal used to secure a vessel to the bed of a body of water to prevent the craft from drifting due to wind or current, girl scouting was an anchor that molded my early childhood years—giving me stability and a place to learn with other girls. As young girls in the late 1960s, we learned how to cook, how to take care of pets, family and home management, and the basics of sewing. I loved arts and crafts and swimming. (If you haven't been able to tell, I really loved swimming!) I was an active child and loved hula hoop and even won a contest for how long I could keep it going. Hopscotch and Chinese jump rope were also favorites. I tried tennis, golf, and water skiing and joined the summer swim team on the naval base. My first years of scouting were with Troop 137 in Pensacola, Florida. I would wear my scout uniform to school because we would stay after school for the scout meeting. I was not embarrassed to wear my uniform. I was *so* proud of it; I even wore it the day of the class picture!

1971—Pensacola, Florida
Alice proudly wore her scout uniform!

After moving back to Hawaii in 1972, I joined Troop 278 with other girls whose families were also in the military. The leaders were military wives, Mrs. Ruth and Mrs. Doane. We were very active, earning badges, camping, hiking, and even having parties (Halloween dress-up) with boys. The leaders were very conscientious and encouraged us to learn the Girl Scout ways. Honesty, respect for authority, and using resources wisely were a few of the Girl Scout laws that I took very seriously. Together, we learned to be courageous and strong while growing through a variety of experiences such as field trips, community service, and environmental protection or conservation. We were taught to plan, budget, and execute what we wanted to do.

1973—Pearl City, Oahu, Hawaii
*Alice accomplished the highest rank
in Girl Scouts, Troop 278—the Gold Award!*

While in the eighth grade, our troop decided we wanted to travel to the Big Island (Hawaii) from Oahu. We set out planning how we would raise the money to take an airplane to another island and stay at a place to see Kilauea Volcano. This would require planning and raising money to fly and stay at the Kilauea Military Camp (KMC), which is within the Hawaiian Volcano National Park.

We collected newspapers and recycled them for money. We did this every month, sometimes twice a month, to raise the funds we needed. We also had a rummage sale (also known as garage sale) at the "Swap Meet" held at the infamous Kam Hi-Way Drive-In Theatre in Aiea. Of course, we sold Girl Scout Cookies and calendars.

In 1974, during our nineth grade year as Cadette Scouts, we embarked on our Big Island trip. We worked hard to make the dream come true. We had a wonderful time on the Big Island. The most memorable thing was getting to hike and being very near a part of the Kilauea volcano that was erupting. I clearly remember a rope barrier that we could go up to but not cross over. Because of an erupting volcano!!! Wow, what an experience of a lifetime.

A very strong remembrance stone was when I learned about lifesaving, and I earned my lifesaving badge and Junior Lifesaving certificate. I decided that I would be a lifeguard one day. Through scouting, I was able to make this dream come true. I would go on to be a lifeguard in the summer after my first year of college. I also worked as a lifeguard all through college at an Olympic-size pool and rotated shifts at the boat dock and a beach, both on the university's campus lake. Swimming was and is still, to this day, my happy place. When I get in the ocean or the pool, I am refreshed in a way that only water can provide. It uplifts me to float, taste the salt, and use my muscles as I glide through the water.

Camping and hiking were other scouting activities I loved. On Oahu, our Troop used US Military Campgrounds. We camped at a place named Camp Smith and at Barbers Point. In scouting, it is common to have a "camp name." I have no idea why I chose my camp name, "Punky." I probably just liked the sound of it. I learned how to plan meals, shop, build a fire, cook on an open fire, be tough in the rain, and how to pack and carry a backpack. As a Troop, we planned and executed a hike on the Waimano Ridge Trail near Pearl City, where we all lived, and ultimately earned our Hiking badge.

Scouting provided opportunities to grow in other areas—outdoor skills, love of nature and the environment, making plans and seeing them to completion, and travel—that would mold me into who I was to become as a grown woman.

Scouting provided an anchor of skills that I would depend on as I moved from childhood into college years, onto being a wife and mother.

HAWAII—THE BEST YEARS

When, as a family, we learned that we would be going back for another duty tour in Hawaii, we were *so* happy! We danced around screaming and shouting for joy. My parents loved Hawaii and island living and their plans were to move back and retire on Oahu.

We first rented a house in Pearl City and then bought a house in Pacific Palisades. School was hard for me. Two major factors made life especially hard for me as a young girl—being a military kid and being a white person. Hawaii is very, very multi-cultured with lots of nationalities: Japanese, Chinese, Filipino, of course, Hawaiian, Samoa, and many Pacific island peoples. So, fitting in was very difficult, and having long blond hair meant not blending in. In middle school, I did a lot of craft classes: sewing, crocheting, and pottery, to name a few. I also loved to cook.

I was also very active in my hula dancing. I took lessons and, in high school, joined a group of dancers, and we performed shows around the island. Participating in the Pearl City High School talent show sophomore year and performing the Tahitian, Māori, and Hula dancing is a wonderful memory. Again, hula dancing was a big part of me.

DRIFTING BEGINS

Military life for us meant my father worked shifts, mostly from eleven p.m. to seven a.m. That meant he was sleeping during the day. We had to be quiet when we returned home from school.

I will probably never know or fully understand exactly what happened during the years between my eighth grade and eleventh grade with my parent's marriage.

My mom began working when I started high school. Now, we had to not only be quiet, but I also had to prepare dinner. It was during these years that I felt lonely and empty. I'm not sure I was so different, being a teenager, attempting to navigate difficult "growing up" feelings and situations, like peer acceptance, friendships, hobbies, my schoolwork, and my time. Or, in my case, *not* navigating well, drifting off course.

Both my parents smoked; mom cigarettes and dad a tobacco pipe. Both drank alcohol, but my father, I remember, always had a beer whenever he was around us. I felt abandoned by my parents and did not feel like I had much guidance or direction. Floating on the current. During these years, nineth to twelfth grades, I began using negative coping habits. I also did not learn how to express my feelings. I was scared! I was scared of not understanding how to handle my feelings. I did try smoking and drinking to cope with these feelings. My parents either were not aware, or they were too busy with marital issues and their own work life. I didn't understand what was happening and again was not able to navigate my feelings in a healthy way. I think the uncertainty of my family unit caused me to look elsewhere to get my teenage needs met.

Whatever the reason, years later, when I became a mother, I realized those coping habits were not the best choices for *my* life!

When my dad was around and I saw him in his military dress uniform, I felt proud, but I was also scared of him. He was the parental disciplinarian. As a middle child, I learned to "read the room." The motto was: Adapt by blending in and not cause conflict. My perception (as a fourteen to seventeen teenage child) of my parents' marriage was that it was not on solid ground. There was tension and arguing. Whether it was the result of the pressure of working nights or too much beer, my father was not present in my life during these years. My mother, while I was happy for her new job and personal growth, did not continue functioning the same as far as taking care of me and my siblings, and the lack of her attention toward me negatively affected me, my brother and sister, and ultimately our entire family.

Overall, these years in Hawaii were positively formative. I loved scouting, the environment, dancing, the ocean, and swimming, and I had a few close friends. But moving around constantly did not provide a firm foundation to make me feel safe. Despite my mom doing her best to keep our family together, I felt our foundation shifting like unstable, shifting sand. I was not only drifting during those last years in Hawaii, but I was about to be pulled into a very strong rip tide.

Just as our family became more rooted in island living, we were about to become uprooted. Again.

> "For I am the Lord your God
> who takes hold of your right hand
> and says to you, Do not fear;
> I will help you."
>
> —Isaiah 41:13 (NIV)

STORMS AND CRASHING WAVES

When my dad got promoted to Master Chief in 1977 and offered the top Naval enlisted position on the base in Guam, how could he turn it down? Move again? I did *not* want to go! I was told by my mother that we were trying to "save" our family. Looking back, in my opinion, my parents should have separated/divorced prior to dragging my sister and I to another island and enduring another move, new school, and new home. My brother had graduated from high school the year before and enlisted in the US Navy, so he was away serving. I was entering my senior year of high school. It's hard to put into words to describe how I felt. Loss. Loss of place, I loved Pearl City High School on Oahu. Loss of the friends I had built and thought I would graduate with.

At that age, kids are all consumed in their own world. I was no different. I think I resented my parents, especially my father, for "making" me leave Hawaii. My closest friend, Lori, went so far as to ask her father if I could live with them, allowing me to stay in Oahu and thus graduate from Pearl City High. My parents said *no*. We needed to stay together. And so I went, feet dragging and not happy when we touched down on the hot tarmac in Tamuning, Guam.

The hot, humid air hit my face with a whoosh. It's funny the things I do remember. There was not a passenger bridge or jetway that connected the gate to the entrance of the plane. Instead, when the humidity knocked me in the face, I walked down those stairs and across the tarmac into my new life in Guam.

THE EBB AND FLOW OF TIDES—GUAM

I'm standing at the edge of the ocean, and the waves are steadily rolling in and out. Like the sun rises every day, I can count on the ebb and flow of the waves. The feeling of my feet sinking slowly deeper into the sand, slowly being covered up, sinking and moving deeper as the water comes in and out. The unsteadiness of which way to turn to pull my feet up and out.

That's the way I felt for the next eighteen months while I was in Guam. Am I going to keep sinking, slowly lose myself, or can I tug and pull my feet up long enough to take a step forward?

Guam is the southernmost island of the Marianas Islands, located near the deepest part of the ocean in the world, the Marianas Trench. The island is small, only thirty miles in length, 8.5 miles wide in the northern tip, and 11.5 miles in the south. Of course, coming from Hawaii, it seemed like the old west, rustic, bush-like, more like a small reef island than a looming volcano. It is much hotter than the Hawaiian islands due to the beautiful trade winds.

My dad bought an old Nissan Datsun, orange, that I drove around the island. I had a few jobs at different times while living there. At one time, I worked at a drugstore as a cashier. Then, at Shakey's Pizza parlor making pizzas, and lastly as a waitress at Pizza Hut.

It was also on Guam that year that I had my one and only ever *cat*.

I can't remember where we got Melvin (the pound we used to say), but I was allowed to have this cat (and the orange Datsun car) since I was uprooted for my senior year of high school. Melvin was an outside cat, gray-striped. He was a fighter and would be out at night and come home in the morning with scratches and cuts.

As far as school on Guam, I loathed going to John F. Kennedy High School. I had a ton of resentment that I was not finishing my high school years at Pearl City High with the friends I had been with since seventh grade. I don't remember studying *at all*! I didn't really make any friends. I had two girls from the Navy base housing that I hung out with and remember going to the Senior "prom" with. My attitude was, "Get through this year and then get off this rock." Needless to say, I was totally unprepared for continuing a higher education, aka college! I was unsure where I was going to go or what I was going to do.

Although my parents tried, they were not able to save their marriage. As a kid, you never really know why your parents divorce. All you really know, no matter what age, is that nothing is ever the same again. I was going to be a daughter of divorced parents.

As much as I try, as an adult and as I was putting these words to paper, I cannot remember a lot of the last six months in Guam. I was in survival mode. I was under a lot of stress caused by my recent graduation and the divorce. Once again, I was moving across the ocean which made me feel on edge and unsettled.

SWEPT OUT TO SEA IN THE RIP CURRENT

As I entered the plane to leave the small island of Guam, I was scared. Like being in an ocean rip current, I was being pulled out, swept away from my family. I was helpless; there was nothing I could do but ride the strong current until its strength released me. The island became a tiny dot as I looked through the small airplane window.

You never know if or when you will get out of the rip current, but I remained calm even though I was frightened of my unknown future. I was eighteen years old and alone on a fifteen-hour flight. The air on the plane was so dry and cold that my nostrils were almost bleeding. I had an entire row of seats to myself; I got blankets, pulled them over my head, and tried to sleep.

The first rule of being in a rip tide current is, "Don't Panic."

I'm not exactly sure how I was able to navigate airports and plane travel alone, but my mother asked me to and, in her own way, had prepared me.

My father remained on Guam after I left in October 1978. Since then, the relationship with my father has been nonexistent. He cut all ties to his family, including his parents, Nana and Grandpa.

Now, at the age of almost sixty-four, and with lots of therapy, I know the divorce was not my fault. However, the lack of 'family' being together, and most importantly, the lack of a relationship with my father, was and is the saddest part of divorce.

Grief is a funny thing; it comes in waves, thankfully, through the years. I have grieved the lack of biological family relationships in a healthy way. God has given me other family and relationships, and most days, I find peace in those gifts.

I became an expert in putting my feelings aside and

performing tasks. Get stuff done. Check items off the list. I was about to embark on one of those tasks that would prove most life-changing.

My parents' divorce left us no choice but for my mother, sister, and I to leave the island of Guam and find a new home. My brother was already in the Navy by this time. So, I had been given a task—flying from Guam to Billings, Montana, by myself to find and rent a house for my mother and sister to live in.

It was November 1978, and I had just turned eighteen the month before. After stopping over and changing flights in Los Angeles, I landed safely in Billings, Montana.

I was greeted at the airport by my Grandpa William Harper (my mom's dad) and quickly went to their house to catch up on sleep after the fifteen hours on an airplane. My mom had done some preliminary work, looking into the availability of houses. I was to meet with the realtor, check out the houses, find a place for us to start our lives over, and get arrangements solidified, like signing a lease and setting up a move-in date. I luckily had success quickly and was able to confirm a place with three bedrooms on a street not too far from where my grandparents lived.

When you are eighteen, you are allowed to join the military, vote, and, of course, drive a vehicle. You are considered an adult. Here I was, being an adult, but it was scary. The worst part was coming from warm island living to cold winter weather! Billings was cold. Arriving with plenty of snow and ice on the ground, I was definitely not in Kansas anymore. I was *not* a snow and winter girl. I was a *sea* and *sand* girl. I was not prepared for the winter. Yes, I liked adventures. But winter. *No!*

At first, I thought, *oh, this is kind of fun*, but I quickly changed my mind. The cold is a hassle. You need a coat, hat, gloves, warm socks, and boots. I didn't have *any* of these after living on tropical islands for the past six years. My mom ordered a coat and boots for me from the JCPenney catalog—a shopping catalog, friends. That's how shopping was done before the internet and Amazon Prime. Ha!

Was I getting any closer to coming out of the now familiar but uncomfortable rip tide? While I enjoyed staying at my grandparents' house for about a month before my mom and sister joined me, I was excited when our new family of three was reunited to celebrate Christmas together. They would form a new beginning in Montana and quickly settled in for the winter. My sister enrolled in high school as a junior.

On the other hand, I did not have a lot of choices regarding what my next steps would be. Going back to Hawaii was an option, but it was determined that it was probably not my best option. Go to college in Billings? I do not remember why my mom did not prefer this option. Ultimately, my mother decided I was to attend Southern Illinois University (SIU) in Carbondale, Illinois (there was also a campus in Edwardsville, Illinois, outside of St. Louis) because I had a relative who lived thirty miles south of Carbondale. Her reasoning was that at least I would have someone nearby in case of emergency. The tides were certainly changing.

I was completely unaware of the life I was about to embark on for the next five and a half years—to attend a university in the middle of the USA. So, I packed my USN military trunk, which had been my father's and was the last remnant of our relationship and once again set out for new beginnings.

> "He is the Maker of heaven and earth,
> the sea, and everything in them—
> He remains faithful forever."
>
> —Psalm 146:6 (NIV)

COMING ASHORE

BUILDING SANDCASTLES

Oftentimes, at the beach, I spent time in the sand, using my feet to dig a hole and finding shells and seaweed to put atop my bucket castles. I used washed-up reed plants to make flags. Burying my sister or her burying me and then pretending we were monsters and slowly pulling, dragging ourselves out of the sand, and running as fast as we could into the waves to rinse off the sand just to do it all over again. The playing and building complicated castles in the sand brought me the peace of knowing I would be okay because this is where I was happy and comfortable.

MY GREAT-GREAT AUNT

Today, I am thankful for relatives, especially my great-great Aunt Mildred Smoot, the sister of my mother's grandfather from Little Rock, Arkansas. She was born in Dongola, Illinois, in July 1909. Aunt Mildred, who had retired by this time in 1979, was a teacher. Years prior, she taught at the University I would be attending.

Lugging my black leather-handled, military footlocker

trunk (later to be used as our college dorm "coffee table"), I left Billings on a cold early morning in January 1979. I flew into Marion, Illinois, where Aunt Mildred and her cousin, Marian, picked me up and drove me to Dongola, Illinois, where she lived.

1979—Dongola, Illinois
*Great-great Aunt Mildred Smoot and
Alice, prior to starting college classes at SIU.*

Her husband, Lowell, had passed away in 1976, the banker of the town of eight hundred and who had, at one time, owned a small oil company. They never had children of their own. My mom talked about Aunt Mildred all the time. Aunt Mildred accepted all her family's children as her own. She took her job as an aunt seriously. My great-grandfather, Leslie Casey, who we called PaPa, was her brother. Growing up, I remember visiting her and thinking she had a lot of money. I don't think she and her husband

Lowell were considered "rich," but they were revered in that small town of eight hundred people. They lived in the only brick home at the top of a hill close to Main Street. Back in the day, the most respected and wealthiest of folks lived in these places, so I guess you could say they were rich.

The town's restaurant, the "Dinner Bell," was the corner daily gathering place, and when I was there for long stretches of time, we would go every day for lunch. The daily specials commonly included things like meatloaf, fried chicken, and catfish—and, of course, dessert. This was the movie-like place to eat, where everyone knew each other, and you could get your big meal of the day, which was called supper. Dinner was what you ate in the evening; supper was lunchtime.

Off we would go, driving down the hill at noon to get our supper. Aunt Mildred had a *big* Lincoln Town car with leather seats—a very nice, fancy car. (Another way people knew she had some money.) We would drive the long two blocks to the Dinner Bell, eat, and sometimes make an appearance at the next-door bank. Aunt Mildred was always dressed very nicely and wore jewelry daily. She also went to the beauty parlor once a week to get her hair washed and "set." So, her hair was always lovely, too. Her skin was milky smooth and soft looking. She would joke around and told me more than once that the reason she didn't have any wrinkles on her face was, "My secret to no wrinkles is to drink a glass of milk every day, which makes me plump so my wrinkles do not show." Aunt Mildred was so sweet and lovable.

Aunt Mildred took me in and treated me as her own child. In the early years of college, during my frequent visits to her house, I stayed in the "Blue Room." Every room in her house was a specific color: Dusty Blue, Rosy Pink. The bathroom was all pink, with pink tile, pink walls, pink towels, and the pink "Dove soap." It smelled lovely in that bathroom, and it was big. But there was no shower, only a bathtub. Aunt Mildred didn't have a shower anywhere in her house. So, I took only baths.

I grew to love her, and I would bring friends and, ultimately, my future husband to pass the "meet Aunt Mildred" visit. All in all, Aunt Mildred was an authentic, loving, and kind person with whom I have fond memories, and I will be forever grateful to her for her steadfastness toward me during my college years.

The years spent in Southern Illinois remind me of building those sandcastles—one bucket of sand at a time, molding and shaping mounds to withstand the sea and wind.

SOUTHERN ILLINOIS UNIVERSITY

I was excited (but scared) to begin college, and looking back, Aunt Mildred went out of her way to make my transition as effortless as she could. In January 1979, after arriving with a lot of snow on the ground, she took me to the bus stop, where I bought a ticket and rode to the SIU Campus. I walked in the snow (with my new boots ordered from the JCPenney clothes catalog) to Woody Hall, where I registered for the spring 1979 semester. I was going to University. From an island girl to a southern girl, little did I know what God had planned for me.

January 1979
Alice arrives at Southern Illinois University.

Since I was not very good at math when I entered college, I began with a review of Algebra and Geometry. No problem.

When I started taking my basic engineering courses, I met the other "girls," young women also studying engineering. We had a few of the basic courses together: Statics, Dynamics, and Fluid Dynamics. We studied together and supported each other. I helped start and was the first President of the Society of Women Engineers (SWE), and we would meet to empower each other.

At the beginning of my sophomore year, our SWE chapter planned a meet-each-other picnic outside by our campus lake near our engineering buildings; the women engineering students and a few guys showed up. One of the guys that came (for the free food) was named Dennis Champagne. He brought a friend with him, and they said they wanted to see us as women succeed in engineering.

We exchanged class schedules and discussed the professors, the good and the bad, especially one in particular who was challenging for everyone. This professor taught my Dynamics class, and being that Dennis seemed very compassionate about my struggle, I asked him if he would help me with the course. He stated that he would. All of us lived and breathed our coursework and really, really supported and encouraged each other through each semester's difficulties and celebrated each other's successes and frustrations.

At that picnic, we played volleyball, and I will always remember Dennis (not only because we have been married for forty years) but because of how funny he was. He walked into the lake to retrieve the ball with his long, bell-bottom jeans and shoes on. Everyone laughed and had a great time. It was a much-needed respite from all our studying. When he walked into the lake, I am not sure why, but that made an impression on me. Carefree spirit? Life of the party? "Go for it" attitude? Helpful and kind by going to get the otherwise never-to-be-seen-again ball?

Maybe all of the above.

That summer, I took Fluid Dynamics, and Dennis was the Teacher's Assistant, better known as TA. Taking classes in the summer was more compact and moved quickly, but they were over in three quarters of the time of a real semester. Dennis was not easy on us, even though we thought a TA would take it easy, *and it was summer*. How hard could it be? Nope, he may have been even harder. But very understanding, and he really wanted us to learn. No one completed the weekly homework or even read the lesson ahead of time for the fluids lab class, so of course, we showed up, and he said, "Pop Quiz." Groans all around. He said, "This is the quiz; *what is the lab about today*? Tell me what we are going to do today." There were more groans as we had not prepared or read the lab before the class. We thought we would read along as we did it. Nope. Preparation for class was important, he said. From that day on, we always read or at least looked at what the lab was going to require of us.

Although Dennis was a few years ahead of me, after the summer of the lab course (which, by the way, I earned an A, and don't laugh, I really did), our friendship grew even more, mostly through his supporting me with the hard engineering course workload.

I worked as a lifeguard at the Olympic-size pool, the boat dock, or the beach on the lake. My schedule worked well with my study load. I needed to work because I needed the money. I enjoyed the work and the other lifeguards became my closest friends. Dennis would come to see me at the boat dock, and we would hang out. We grew closer, started dating, and eventually fell in love. He graduated with a master's degree in 1983 and began working in Florissant, Missouri, as an aircraft engineer at McDonnell Douglas Aerospace Corporation.

During the first few summers of college, my mom flew me back to Montana, where I worked to save money for college expenses. The first summer, I was a lifeguard and a waitress. The second summer, and by then, I had declared environmental engineering as my major, my mom made a connection and I applied for a job at the Bridger Coal Company—a coal mine in Wyoming. I was accepted and she also found through a connection a room to rent in the town of Rock Springs, closest to where I had to drive to work. It was a thirty-three-mile one-way drive from where I rented this room to get to my job each day.

I was employed as a Reclamation Technician. The coal mine was a strip coal mine, not an underground mine. It is legally required to reclaim or revegetate the land after mining, planting plants, and irrigating so vegetation would return.

1980—Bridger Coal Company
Summer job—The PHD's—Pipe Hauling Detail Crew! (Alice center)

I was required to wear a hard hat and steel-toed boots! It was hot, too. Our small team of four college kids hauled irrigation pipes and monitored vegetated plots and animal counts. We called ourselves the PHD's—Pipe Hauling Detail! This was an adventurous summer job, one that I will never forget!

SISTERS OF MY HEART

After arriving at Southern Illinois University (SIU) with my military trunk and enrolling in classes, I began to make friends in my dorm.

Dorm life was fun. When we were not studying, we would go to each other's rooms and hang out. The eleventh floor of the Mae Smith Tower, where I resided, planned activities for the girls on that floor. That's how I met most of my first friends.

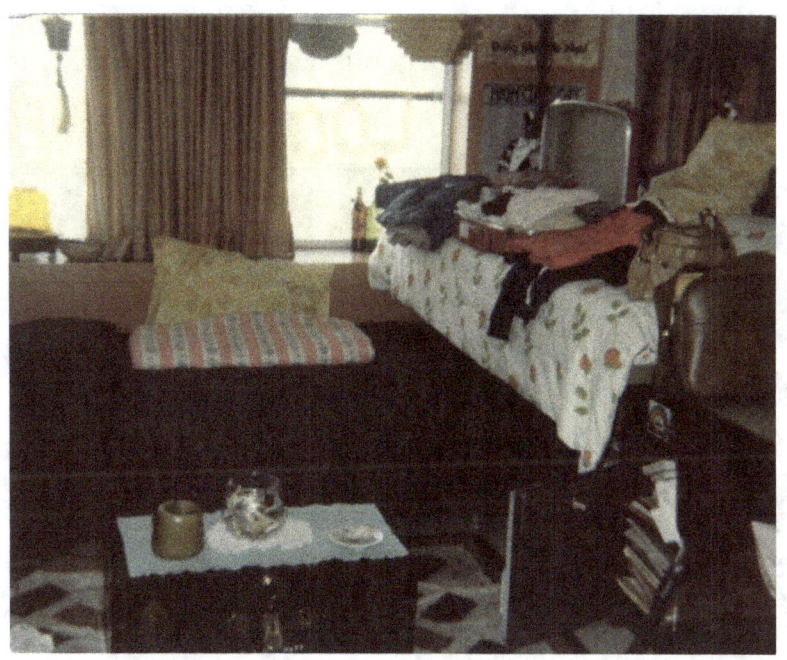

Southern Illinois University, Mae Smith Tower
Alice's dad's military trunk makes a great coffee table for her dorm room life.

When I enrolled at SIU, I did not know anyone to choose for a roommate, so it was a roll of the dice. Needless to say, my roll was not a pleasant one. My first roommate was Leona from Pittsburg, Pennsylvania. She didn't study, slept all day, locked me out of the room, and drank a lot of alcohol. This situation helped me find my sister of the heart, Lynn Gross. She lived down the hall, and we became instant besties. The next semester (Fall 1979), we roomed together, and we agreed we were sisters of the heart, which means God-given or a sister from God rather than biological.

Since my mother lived in Montana, it was not easy to "go home," and I was unable to make that trip often. Lynn's parents "adopted" me as their own, as their fourth daughter, and I became a member of the Gross Family. They were from the south side of Chicago. Jack and Kitty Gross, Lynn, Denise, and Jackie. And as a bonus, I got their grandparents, too.

*The Gross Family with
Alice and Dennis at their wedding–with Lynn Gross
(Maid of Honor) and her parents, grandparents, and siblings.*

For many, many years, college and after, I would visit Lynn and her family. As we grew older, I got married, and we had our careers and children. Lynn continued to live in Chicago, and when we went to visit Dennis' family, I would say I needed to visit my family, heading over to see her. We still talk and visit each other.

That 1979 spring semester forever changed me, and I am forever grateful for her in my life. Her family is my family, and my family is her family. We may not get to choose our biological family, but God sure does provide others to stand in that gap. We have had many adventures together, and I am hopeful that there will be many more.

Another sister-of-the-heart is my friend Lisa. We "get" each other. Some people who know us call us "the same person." We laugh and hug and say, "Yep, we are." You know, "the person" who cares about you no matter what happens? That's us. We met at St. Thomas Lutheran Church when our kids were in grade school and have been friends for thirty years. She and her husband, Jake, have been with Dennis and I through our darkest and brightest days.

For those other sisters of mine—too many to name, but you know who you are—I love each of you. Your friendship and our walk together through life are a balm to my soul. You mean the world to me.

To my one and only sister, Melinda, I am sorry I wasn't there for you when we left Guam, and you were with Mom alone. Years later, you moved to take care of Mom in her dying days. I want to be there for you as your big sister. I'm thankful for our recent reconnection and am reminded that sisters, real sisters, must work just as hard for a healthy and long-lasting relationship. Playing games outside, riding our bikes, playing with dolls, and "hang heads" are just a few of my happiest memories made with you. I hope to make more memories together!

I do not take for granted any of my sister relationships and think about how to connect and love each of you the best I am able.

My sister's rock of remembrance is one I will cherish forever.

BEING AN AUNTIE

Thirty-three years after those notable years in Southern Illinois and with my great-great Aunt Mildred, I would be called upon to open my doors to be an Auntie to one of my nephews. It was 2012 now, and years had passed since I had walked through the snow at SIU in January 1979. I received a phone call from my niece, Charsy, the eldest of my brother's children. Her dad, my brother, was unable to take care of her youngest brother, Matthew, age thirteen at the time. My brother had addiction problems and was having difficulties, as often is the cyclic nature of addiction.

My children didn't hesitate when we, as a family, came together in an emergency-type meeting to figure out how to help. "We have to bring him here," they said. Three days later, he flew from Pensacola, Florida, to Atlanta. Marietta, Georgia, became home to him even though I spent the next few months trying to convince my brother that he had what it takes to be a supporting father and that if he got himself help for his drinking problem, he could raise his son himself. My brother disagreed, and six weeks later, we became legal guardians for Matthew, enrolled him in eighth grade, and took a trip to Florida to get the rest of his personal belongings.

Throughout the next five years and then four years of college, both Uncle Dennis and I gave our entire support to raise this young man. I, as his Auntie, felt like his mother. We prayed that we could be good "parents" one more time. Our children had been out of the house for over ten years by then.

We embraced everything again—marching band, Boy Scouts, needing a car or rides to activities, and choosing a college, to name a few. Like my Aunt Mildred, I did what I needed to help in the success of not only a relative but someone we loved.

My brother passed away just two years after Matt came to live permanently with us. Whew, that was one of our hardest days, having to tell him his dad had passed away. Despite my brother's problems, he *loved* his children. He called Matt, wrote him letters, and called me to see how he was doing. He expressed his thanks to us for helping raise him. My brother loved Jesus despite his long sufferings, and I know his children have learned to know the Lord as well. I know this would make their dad happy on earth. We are so proud of who Matt has become. He earned his Eagle Scout rank, and he graduated college with a music Ed degree, just to name a few things we are proud of for him. He is, as Uncle Dennis claims, a productive member of society, and we pray he is happy.

It never occurred to me in 1979, when great-great Aunt Mildred picked me up from Marion airport, me hauling that military trunk, that I, in turn, would pick up my nephew and his trunk and help him navigate along life's pathways. Strange as it may sound, the sandcastles I built may each look different as I made them, but it's in the molding and shaping that we learn what may work and what might not. Each piece of shell decoration and sand tunnel helped me learn to adjust what I needed in that moment.

MY BEST FRIEND

I graduated from college in May 1984, and Dennis and I were married on June 23, 1984.

June 23, 1984—Elmhurst, Illinois
Wedding Day of Dennis James Champagne and Alice Jeanne Martratt.

At that time, President Ronald Reagan was in office (1981–1989), and the environmental issues in America became more bipartisan. The Reagan administration and their proponents claimed there was excessive environmental regulation, and thus, many laws were deregulated. The 1980s brought environmental justice due to people fighting back when PCB-laden soil was going to be buried in their community.

I say all this because when I graduated, finding a job in environmental protection was impossible, especially with little to no experience. The country was in the middle of a big recession and all-time high unemployment. I used my lifeguard and retail skills until I ended up with an engineering planning job at McDonnell Douglas, where Dennis also worked. Not my ideal situation but it allowed Dennis and I to start our family and earn enough income to buy our first house.

After Dennis and I got married and we settled into life in St. Louis, both of us working at McDonnell Douglas, we found out we were expecting our first child.

We were so excited when we had a girl, Rene Elizabeth. Two years later, we had John Tyler. God blessed us with two children, and we love them so much. We have enjoyed creating and experiencing memories throughout the years with our family.

1990—Florissant, Missouri
The Champagne Family—Dennis and Alice,
Rene Elizabeth (age four), and John Tyler (age two).

We lived in St. Louis from 1984–1991. These were good years for our early marriage and family of four. Dennis had been working for almost ten years on a few military airplane designs and was intrigued by a next-generation aircraft design program. I was used to relocating because of my nomadic childhood, and now I had been in one place for seven years! Unheard of. Let's go.

He interviewed for jobs in Seattle, Washington (Boeing), and Marietta (Atlanta), Georgia (Lockheed Martin). Our relocating considerations were: if we moved to Seattle, we would be closer to Hawaii, where my mother and sister had moved back to and were now living. But, when he went to Marietta to interview and consider moving there, he said it was a better cost of living, and he received a much better job offer. When I went to visit Georgia, I fell in love with the landscape. The City of Atlanta, affectionately known as "a city in a forest," has hills, lots of green trees and flowers, and is warm. I loved Georgia, *and* this new home would be closer to the ocean, which I desperately needed because my body required Vitamin Sea!

With the decision locked in, we moved to Marietta, Georgia, in the fall of 1991, when the children were ages three and five, and Dennis joined Lockheed Martin, where he would remain for the next twenty-nine years.

Moving to Georgia was one of the greatest decisions we made. We enjoy living here very much and fully access all the things around us to explore. The entire Southeast, the Georgia coast, Florida, mountains; we have traveled to a lot of places near us.

Raising our family in one place and not moving every three to four years was unusual for me, but I was so very happy to stay in one place. We have now been in our house since October 31, 1991. I never thought I would ever live in the same place this long!

After all of the moving around, God finally planted me/us, and it has been amazing. Dennis is the best part of my life, my best friend, and everything I could have hoped or dreamed of and more to have in a loving husband. We have been through a lot, as most married couples do. Our marriage focus is keeping our eyes on Jesus as we are transformed daily and attempt to live and keep in step with the Spirit.

We raised our children, Rene and John, who are both married now with children of their own. We are grandparents, and we think that's the best job in the world! I pray every day for all the grands and know that He is faithful throughout all generations. I'm positive my Grandpa and Nana Martratt would be smiling down if he could see all his great and great-great-grandchildren.

I think about God's unfailing love and faithfulness that continues to each generation, and I am trusting and confident that it will continue.

> "But the fruit of the Spirit is love, joy, peace, forbearance, kindness, goodness, faithfulness, gentleness and self-control. Against such things, there is no law. Those who belong to Christ Jesus have crucified the flesh with its passions and desires. Since we live by the Spirit, let us keep in step with the Spirit."
>
> —Galatians 5:22-25 (NIV)

MOANA

FIRM FOUNDATION

When we moved to Hawaii (for the second time) in 1972, I was twelve years old. My brother was fourteen and starting high school. I started seventh grade, and my sister started fifth grade. When I got to nineth grade in 1974, my brother was a Junior. I looked up to my brother. He was cool! He wore his hair long and flowing, a style popular in the '70s surfer hair. He wore cool Hawaiian shirts and played the guitar! At an early age, I followed "Bubba," as I called him, around, and in high school, I continued but from afar.

Because my mom was a working mom and my father worked nights, we were often left to our own devices. Since we grew up watching our dad drinking beer, we did that too. Same with smoking cigarettes. Needless to say, these high school years were tough. As a kid, you know things are not right, but you don't know exactly what's wrong. Whether because of marriage, health, or excess alcohol problems, it was during these years that our family grew apart.

My dad, who, in my memory, was always working, drank a lot. Beginning in nineth grade, I was lonely, lost my direction, and turned inward because I did not know how to communicate my feelings, feel safe, or get my needs met. Maybe it was my fourteen-year-old self's way of survival. I did not know how to deal with my parents and the situation we found ourselves in—growing apart, arguing, and everyone going their own way.

I'm not proud of some of my behavior and often wonder how I survived some of the things Lori and I did back then. Lori was the friend I hung out with regularly. Her dad was an air traffic controller and worked nights, too, and slept all day. Her mom died at the end of our eighth-grade year, and she had to take care of her sister and also dealt with a dad who wasn't present. So, the two of us were really on our own, so to speak.

I presume now that although I felt hurt and lost and struggled to navigate growing up without a lot of guidance, I had a firm foundation in my very being, a strength that God planted many years before. Whether from growing up in a family with excessive alcohol use or being a middle child, I did not learn how to express my feelings or process them, and denial of those feelings was what I thought I was doing for much of my life.

NO REGRETS

I now understand what I thought was the denial of my thoughts and feelings was really *survival*. Denial is construed as a negative behavior when consciously selecting to reject the truth. Survival is not a choice but rather a way to live and get through whatever is happening at that particular time. I didn't cause the adverse life things that happened to me—divorced parents, abandoned by my earthly father, and having to figure things out in Southern Illinois—but I did survive them, and God walked beside me every step. During the lowest moments of those years of survival living, my determination was growing. Little by little, I experienced positive, life-giving, God-given mercies as He shined a light on my path. Instead of looking down, I choose to look up and trust in the one who created the universe and knows every star by name.

> "I lift up my eyes to the mountains—
> where does my help come from?
> My help comes from the Lord,
> the Maker of heaven and earth.
> He will not let your foot slip—
> he who watches over you will not slumber;
> indeed, he who watches over Israel
> will neither slumber nor sleep.
> The Lord watches over you—
> the Lord is your shade at your right hand;
> the sun will not harm you by day,
> nor the moon by night.
> The Lord will keep you from all harm—
> he will watch over your life;
> the Lord will watch over your coming and going
> both now and forevermore."
>
> —Psalm 121 (NIV)

My mother was an example to me that women can do anything. At the age of forty-three, she graduated from college with a nursing degree. We graduated the same year! She often encouraged me to be all that I could be and not be afraid to try new things.

During the years my mom lived in Georgia, I strived for a healthy relationship with my mother. I attempted to be a good daughter and be everything that I thought mattered to her. This meant inviting her to dinner, going to her house, helping her with chores, pretty much anything, but I felt like I never measured up. I could never do enough, never be good enough. No matter what I did, she was not happy with me.

After years of counseling and asking, is it me? What did I do? I realized, deep in my soul, that it was not me. Through prayer and study, I started to believe what God says about me. I *am* loved. I *am* significant. Two important affirmations children long to hear and know deep down from their parents. You could say it was her past—you could say it was her parents—I don't know. I believe she had a lot of wounds that affected her mental health. Wounds that she chose either to ignore or not get help for the hurts they caused.

Through counseling, I learned the phrase, "Hurt people, hurt people." I also learned that if you are alive, then you probably have hurts, habits, and hang-ups. It is what we do about them that matters. I continue to go to counseling and refer to my appointments as my "mental health check-ups." Ultimately, I realize that no matter what I could've done to change the circumstances, I must do what is best and healthy for me and my family.

Being part of a family is hard. Navigating others' feelings, receiving and giving affirmations, and ultimately forgiving each other on a daily basis is necessary.

In 2011, I was diagnosed with a brain tumor (more on this later). During this particular time, my mother and I were not on the best terms, better known as "the not speaking to each other" years. When Dennis informed her about the scheduled brain surgery, I chose to tell her, "It's okay, you do not need to come and be here with me." She never forgave me for my decision not to allow her to be with me for my brain surgery, which, most importantly by the way, was successful. The benign meningioma was half the size of a tennis ball. In my mind, I just couldn't handle another thing. Was now the time to pretend that our relationship was okay? I could not.

I am told forgiveness is not for the person you are forgiving of whatever they did to you, but rather for yourself so that you aren't eaten up with bitterness.

Two of my guy friends from work came to visit me while I was recovering. I knew they were trying to cheer me up when one of them made a comment I thought was hilarious. When I proudly displayed the line of huge staples across my skull, along with my new haircut (not), the reaction to seeing my trauma was diffused and summed up by one friend saying, "Wow! You had brain surgery! That is way cooler and even better than being shot." You had to be there.

Nevertheless, four years later, when another horrible health struggle came for my body, I never heard from my mother.

When she became ill, she did not inform me of the seriousness of her health issues, nor was I asked to help her.

I am thankful my sister was asked and decided to move to Pensacola, Florida, after residing years in Portland, Oregon, to take care of our mom. Right or wrong, due to the boundaries that I formed, she was not caring toward me or my family for the last ten years of her life. I didn't feel loved anyway, so when she died in 2020, I recognized I had already spent years grieving the lack of a relationship with her, although I was sad that she passed away.

Remember in the beginning when I mentioned digging down to feel my feelings? Feeling unloved was hard to admit to myself. I spent a lot of time on my knees, asking

God to redeem our relationship. God knew in my heart that I wanted a healthy relationship with my mother. Could I have done things differently? Possibly. But in the end, my mother's inability to recognize her part in our relationship, whether from an undiagnosed mental illness or her not wanting a relationship with her daughter, prevented that from happening, and to this day, I have no regrets. No regrets. Yes, my mom was a strong woman, but not strong enough to love me like God does; loved beyond measure.

> "And may you have the power to understand, as all God's people should, how wide, how long, how high, and how deep his love is."
>
> —Ephesians 3:18 (NLT)

WOMAN POWER!

During high school between 1972 and 1976, with the foundation that my mother gave me, skills from scouting, traveling, and the love of the environment, I decided (despite feeling lost, lonely, and unloved) that I would *be* something. I would get a job a woman could be *strong* at. Not a secretary or a teacher, not that there is anything wrong with those jobs, but during this time period, these were typical women's jobs. *No*, I wanted to be different. I didn't think about having a family or being a mother. I wanted to be a leader. I desired to accomplish things as a woman and support and encourage other women. Scouting gave me this drive as we had a sisterhood. I wanted goals and growth as I grew older. I had a never-stop learning mindset.

I guess you could say I was a young women's movement participant. Growing up in the 1960s, I saw women fighting for equality. The basic goals women were focused on (and in some ways still are) were equal rights and discrimination. These included equal pay for equal work, putting an end to domestic violence, equal rights in managerial jobs, ending sexual harassment, and sharing of responsibility in housework and raising children. Most people want to be valued and have a vital role. Aware of all these social changes as a girl, I wanted to be more than a housewife.

Growing up in Hawaii during these years established my love for the environment. The Hawaiian culture cares deeply about the protection of its natural resources. The ocean, mountains, and land are considered sacred. My love for the environment and the social movements I had witnessed during that time influenced my decision to focus on environmental engineering (even though I was not strong in math, nor was I prepared from high school math). (So, Lilly and James, if you are reading this, study, study, study, and learn that math!)

Sheer determination and perseverance were what I had!

Graduating from high school in 1978, I wanted to focus on alternative energy, like solar energy. The 1973 Oil Embargo made a huge impact on me. "Alternative energy resources— come on, people, we need to do better," were my thoughts. My college courses were taken from the School of Thermal and Environmental Engineering. It's like Civil Engineering, but I call it a hybrid. During my career, I focused on water— stormwater, drinking water, soil erosion and sedimentation, flood management, as well as community impacts on local streams. Design of wastewater treatment plants, power plants, water plants, and energy systems are just a few examples of topics I studied in my pursuit of this degree.

1978 — Tamuning, Guam
Alice Jeanne Martratt, high school graduation.

God placed desires in my heart for a reason. I am filled with gratitude as I visualize myself placing a huge stone of remembrance regarding my life purpose (by the way, we can have more than one!), not only taking steps to figure out what these desires were (working to help the environment) but also ways to activate them.

"Teach me to do your will,
for you are my God.
May your gracious Spirit lead me forward
on a firm footing."

—Psalm 143:10 (NLT)

PILINA (SPECIAL CONNECTIONS)

I think most women want and love adventures of all sorts. I know I do. Whether it's owning your own business, being a mother, traveling the world, riding a motorcycle, biking down Haleakala volcano, or sewing a dress, God gives each of us a calling or purpose. With each season of life, your purpose can change. I believe that we need to live out these purposes with others—in community. We are given the desire deep within us to share adventures. To "do life with others." God made us to connect.

I learned that women need other women to help us process our goals and connect us to others. For me, one of these women is Sally Bethea, whom I met in 1992 after moving to Marietta, Georgia, the year before.

Sally and I met at the Georgia Conservancy, where she was employed. I wanted to volunteer and get my foot in the door at an environmental protection company. My dream job was working for the US Environmental Protection Agency, which I did have a few interviews in the late '80s and early '90s to no avail.

A volunteer coordinator paired me with Sally, who initially gave me small tasks to help her out, and over the next several months, she encouraged me to keep coming. One day, she asked me to attend a meeting. A group of influential people (Ted Turner's daughter, husband, and a few others) were hosting a meeting to discuss starting a group to help protect the Chattahoochee River that flows from north Georgia through Atlanta emptying into the Gulf of Mexico at Apalachicola Bay.

It was during this meeting of about forty people, a lot of whom had significant experience in environmental work in Atlanta, that I experienced God's presence. It's a fluttering feeling in your body; it's the Holy Spirit nudging and a bravery that can't come from me alone. That's how you know it's God. At that meeting, I went up to the now Co-Founder of Chattahoochee Riverkeeper and told him that I wanted to be the Assistant to the Riverkeeper. He told me to talk to Sally.

I didn't know that night, but Sally was a lead candidate to be the Executive Director and Riverkeeper of the new organization and was ultimately selected. I volunteered to help her start this new organization, assisted her in setting up the office, and became the first employee, Assistant to the Riverkeeper, in 1993. I brought an old phone from my basement storage room to our newly rented space, and we went to a Goodwill and bought two blue chairs and began this new journey.

One of our biggest success stories was filing a federal lawsuit using the Clean Water Act of 1972 against the City of Atlanta. For decades, the under-designed and under-capacity sewage treatment for the millions of Atlantans allowed raw sewage to flow into the Chattahoochee River, the drinking water for almost three million people. Fresh, clean water was to be fought for and protected for future generations. *Keeping the Chattahoochee*, a book Sally would later go on to write, describes a lot of the early years of our efforts.

My strength was God's strength. Was it easy? No. Did I

have a lot of doubts? Incredibly, a *lot*! But I was pioneering something new. It was exciting to be blazing a trail. Sally was a remarkable example of encouragement to me as a young woman.

Determination and perseverance! These are two of the strongest qualities I have and still believe in as I write these words.

I had many experiences working at the Chattahoochee Riverkeeper organization. One of the most memorable was as a Georgia Registered Lobbyist. Every year, the Georgia General Assembly, the state lawmakers, meet to pass laws, amend laws, or hold hearings. As a registered lobbyist, I was to influence lawmakers to protect the Chattahoochee River. Educating others about the importance of the river as the major drinking water source was paramount to understanding our organization's position of protecting the river. My expertise was focused on riparian buffers, erosion and sediment control, and stormwater management. We often found ourselves frustrated and disillusioned, but we never gave up. Learning to navigate political viewpoints, communicate position statements, and strong networking with like-minded individuals would help us reach our goals and were lobbying skills I mastered.

I worked with Sally for thirteen years. We were literally fighting battles to protect the river—the lifeblood and drinking water now for over six million people. Without water (clean water to drink), we cannot exist. The top contributor of pollution to the river at this time was sediment from stormwater runoff from construction sites. Atlanta was in a growing boom. Clearing of trees and new construction was everywhere you looked. We received a research grant, hired a consultant to perform a scientific study, and published a report about this number one issue damaging the river.

We discovered there were locally elected and appointed members to a Board termed the Soil and Water Conservation Districts. The Boards are comprised of local citizens who work to protect their community's land and water resources. It was legally formed in 1935, following the infamous "Dust Bowl," which hurt much of America's heartland by landowners clearing land and causing harmful erosion. The locally elected boards play an important role in our work at the CRK. We learned who these folks were and began to befriend those whom we knew their hearts were about environmental protection. The opposition was those who appointed and elected folks who had their own personal desires to see development. People like local developers and their own county officials sitting on the same board approving construction plans from companies they had ties to. Sally approached me to become a candidate for the Cobb County Soil and Water Conservation District (SWCD) in 2000. With only twenty-five signatures required to qualify and endorsed by the Sierra Club, I was off and running to defeat my "developer opponent." I was the "protect our resources" candidate, not "develop the resources." I won the election and was sworn in as an elected State of Georgia official in January 2000, the same year I turned forty years old.

2000—Powder Springs, Georgia
*Alice was elected to the Cobb Soil and
Water Conservation District on the platform of
stream protection, serving through 2016, a total of sixteen years.*

For my third term, I was on the Cobb County November ballot with US Presidential nominee Barack Obama. Woot! I remained on the SWCD Board until 2016 when I decided not to run for office again.

Protecting the river from dirt was a big job! Development was rampant in the Metro Atlanta area. Because it was determined through a scientific study that erosion from construction sites washing off during storms was the number one pollutant to the river, the Chattahoochee was also deemed one of the top ten most endangered rivers in the US. We had our work cut out for us. I helped create what went on to receive multiple awards, an Erosion and Sediment Control Manual, and a Workbook for Citizens called *Get the Dirt Out*. I assisted to develop the materials, including a Field Guide, a Checklist, and a Site Report Card, and trained thousands of people throughout the State of Georgia and beyond. Presenting this material at local and National conferences, assisting Riverkeeper attorneys in filing lawsuits as well as training additional trainers on how to monitor and report activities at construction sites ultimately resulted in my nomination for a National Award.

In 2005, I received one of five in the nation River Hero Awards, for my effort in the *Get the Dirt Out* program.

2005—Colorado
Alice proudly showing her River Hero Award.

Here's what the River Network organization said:

"Alice Champagne, Technical Programs Director, Upper Chattahoochee Riverkeeper. Alice has worked tirelessly for over a decade on the Chattahoochee River's most serious problem—polluted sediment runoff from construction sites in the sprawling metro Atlanta region. Never afraid to speak up at public meetings, to lead and teach citizen and governmental trainings/workshops, or to challenge proposed development plans that may negatively impact the river, she is considered the erosion and stormwater expert in the state's environmental community."

My award hangs on my wall where I can look at it every day. It is an unforgettable rock of remembrance.

A few years before I left Riverkeeper, I began feeling another Holy Spirit nudge. My time at Riverkeeper, while I loved every minute, was coming to an end. I wanted to be a manager. Be careful of what you ask for! Through my network of women water managers and engineers, I found out about a job opening at the City of Roswell, Georgia. I applied and got hired as a water resources engineer. I quickly got up to speed on local government operations and completed projects that had been unfinished since the departure of the previous division manager. In addition to performing the duties of the engineer, I also operated as the interim Water Resources Division Manager. Although I did not hold the qualifications of the necessary Professional Engineer (P.E.) certification, I was doing the job out of necessity and my strong capabilities from my previous jobs at Riverkeeper.

One day, after being in the bathroom with the door locked, praying, "Jesus, help me," I walked into my Department Head's office and proceeded to tell him that I was intended to be the Water Resources Manager and that despite what he thought, God told me I was going to have this position. Was I crazy, losing my mind? My boss agreed, began the changes to the job description, and I was promoted within a few months. Ultimately, I brought the division up to meet the State and Federal law requirements as well as receiving several grants and awards. I led and managed four direct employees and fifteen overall. I respected that job and the people I worked with.

I began the City position just as I was beginning to volunteer with an organization called Living Water International (LWI). In 2007, I attended a Passion conference where I learned about the non-profit that drills wells for clean water in Central American communities, such as Guatemala, Honduras, Nicaragua, and El Salvador.

My first well-drilling trip was to Honduras in 2009. This lit a fire in me to recruit others—from my church and from my water profession—to come alongside me, raise funds, and build more wells. Thus began the journey with LWI, where I organized, managed, and led multiple fundraising efforts to raise awareness of the need for clean water in undeveloped countries and recruit teams to go on trips to drill the wells and provide education to the community. Ultimately, I went on nine trips to Central American countries between 2009 and 2018.

2014—Nicaragua
*Alice and Dennis with Stonebridge church members
celebrating the successful clean water well for the community.*

I was hopeful about obtaining a paid position with LWI in Atlanta with the opening of a new office. However, the economy had other plans, and the office never opened. I remained at the City job and was promoted again to the position of Deputy Director for the Environmental/Public Works Department, serving over one hundred employees and large community. I was blessed to "retire" in 2018, and happy to leave behind and detox from a day-to-day multitasker, list checker, and go-go calendar doer to a "where can I serve today" mindset.

My strength of determination was and remains one of my greatest attributes to this day. I am so grateful for this strength, which I have used repeatedly throughout my life.

The same year I was first elected, I earned a black belt. My son John and I attended classes and practiced together. At the ages of sixteen and forty, we accomplished something only one out of one thousand people can say they have done. We trained for five years to obtain a first-degree black belt in Karate. *Wow!* The determination! The strength and courage I had to be strong. That same thirteen-year-old girl, whose mother drove her and picked her up in the dark in Aiea, Hawaii, to earn a Lifesaving Certification, was now a black belt.

The sheer will that steered me then and continues today is something I will always cherish and be forever thankful God made me this way.

Being elected to that Board in 2000 was a gift and a stone of remembrance.

I can look back now and see God's faithfulness to me, but this wasn't always the case.

⁵ "I am the vine; you are the branches. If you remain in me and I in you, you will bear much fruit; apart from me you can do nothing. ⁶ If you do not remain in me, you are like a branch that is thrown away and withers; such branches are picked up, thrown into the fire and burned. ⁷ If you remain in me and my words remain in you, ask whatever you wish, and it will be done for you. ⁸ This is to my Father's glory, that you bear much fruit, showing yourselves to be my disciples."

—John 15:5-8 (NLT)

FAITHFUL IN THE CURRENT

I grew up going to church on holidays or in grade school, and I remember Mom taking me to Sunday School classes or vacation Bible school. It seemed important to her to go to church, but now, as an adult, I am not entirely sure why. I have no memories of learning *about* God or who Jesus was. My parents were not religious. I was taught mealtime prayers, but did they pray with me? No. Whether it was for show or they thought they should, I think they started out taking us to a Lutheran church to learn about God. Somewhere between the time frame of eighth and nineth grade, we simply stopped going. There was no explanation that I can recall. But the family started to experience what I now know as dysfunction—beginning with communication.

In the Martratt family, talking about our feelings was not something we did. We simply didn't talk about things. I learned to observe. I have vague recollections of my mom telling me, "Dad doesn't feel well," or "Dad's sleeping." Was he ill? Was it excessive alcohol? I will never know.

But I missed going to church. I was very disappointed and embarrassed years later that I did not get to participate in an event called Confirmation. After two years of classes and the end of eighth grade, I was told I would be able to publicly profess my faith in Jesus. I did neither. I didn't complete the classes or get the "confirmation." As a young girl, I thought that I lacked something important because I didn't get to complete this Christian education. Years later, I gave this hurt to the Lord and was lifted of this guilt.

After Dennis and I were married in Chicago in a Lutheran church, we did not attend church at all. Then, when we had Rene, I felt the Holy Spirit telling me to find a church. I wanted to find a church home and family.

One day, I happened to be driving by a church, and God took control of my life by taking control of my car. I had driven by this church previously, as the road it was on was a road we had taken often to get around town. It was a weekday—and my car literally drove into the parking lot of the church. I got out and went in and talked to the pastor. Shortly thereafter, our little family started attending that church, Christ the King Lutheran Church in Florissant, Missouri.

Both children were baptized there, and we enjoyed that church family for the seven years we were in St. Louis. I was active there with the women's small group (Ruth Circle) Bible study and the larger women's group (WELCA—Women of the Evangelical Lutheran Church America) and was greatly influenced by a number of women there who helped me to learn more about Jesus and grow stronger in God's word. I felt God's love probably for the first time at this church, and I am thankful to this day that God didn't give up on me and that I chose to seek Him too. It was a precious and sweet time—just the thing Dennis and I both needed to begin our family's journey with a church family.

When we moved from St. Louis to Marietta, we found a church family right away. I cherished what I had learned about God to this point and wanted more. I also wanted my children to grow up and learn more about God and Jesus than I had. We continued to attend church, worship with other believers, study the Bible, and connect with others. We are not created to be alone. Seeking God and seeing glimpses of God's faithfulness during these years were very rewarding and necessary.

> [11] "For I know the plans I have for you," declares the Lord, "plans to prosper you and not to harm you, plans to give you hope and a future. [12] Then you will call on me and come and pray to me, and I will listen to you. [13] You will seek me and find me when you seek me with all your heart."
>
> —Jeremiah 29:11-13 (NIV)

BROKEN PIECES

Have you ever walked along the ocean shoreline looking for shells, but all you find are broken pieces?

It's super hard to find a whole, intact shell. When I am looking, I usually find broken ones. Occasionally, I may find a whole one with no edges missing. The feeling I receive is one of joy when I find an intact shell. Can you imagine how God feels when one of His children has more healing from knowing how we are created for His purpose? I imagine it's how I feel when I find an intact shell.

Being whole takes many forms. Going to counseling for some. Reading the Bible. Having a friend that you can talk to about anything. Sometimes, you need to go backward before going forward. Let me explain. A defining moment in my life was getting on the plane with my military trunk and flying to Southern Illinois.

That was the point when I knew my life was going to be different. I made a decision on that plane that change would be beneficial. This was a new beginning and a change of the tide.

I must let go of the past and accept who I am.

I find my strength in all the changes and rhythms that have shaped me. The result of all the childhood moves, disruptions of divorce, and pain of leaving the familiar and friends behind are all the pieces of me that were painful and I considered a weakness. But these changes are what shaped me.

The piece of the past that I needed to let go of was the part of wanting a mom and dad who loved me. A mom and dad that had a house I could go home to. The pain I felt in my early 20s of not having a home to go to and a father who abandoned me was more pain than I could bear at that time.

During my senior year of high school and while I was doing my own teenage thing, my parent's marriage was completely unraveling. My father had an affair, and at one point, my mother was hospitalized for a "mental breakdown." Of course, we didn't talk about it. So, I pushed down my feelings more and more.

The hurt just kept piling on. My parents divorced, and my father stayed in Guam (and is still living there today). Over the next several decades, the family dynamic would splinter even more as we all went our separate ways. I went to Montana and, ultimately, Southern Illinois, Florissant, Missouri, and then Georgia. My mom went to Montana, Hawaii, Georgia, and then Florida. My sister went to Montana, Hawaii, and Oregon and now lives in Florida. My brother, who had joined the Navy, went to a remote Pacific Island, Pohnepei, where he lived and worked for many years. He moved his family to Georgia and then Florida.

During my college years, I saw my father only once. Then I saw him just a few times between the late '80s and late '90s. He didn't give me away at my wedding (remember that was Grandpa Martratt).

1984
Grandpa Martratt giving Alice away at her wedding.

He didn't come to my brother's funeral. In 2023, I asked (through a message to his wife) if I could visit him in Guam. Sadly, he declined.

Although my mom provided a place to "go home" after I first went to college, after she graduated, she started moving around, too. But then I got married and started my own home.

I built up a survivor wall so thick it would take a sledgehammer to chip away hurts for years! Now, I accept that my parents did the best they could. I accept that God planted me where I needed to be. He had a plan for my life, even though I could not see it. He had me in the palm of His hand the entire time. And still does.

I made a decision to go backward so that I could go forward. To look at my childhood memories and discover a freedom in them that God never left me. The way I grew up, moving around, however painful it was, is what made me unique.

Looking back at all the memories, reaching and grasping the good parts, and letting go of the painful parts to write this book provides me freedom from the past! Free of the hurts of the past that I let grip places of my heart that God wanted to fill. Just as the tides come in and wash afresh the sands and shape the shore, God wants to wash our pains away. God's love, when we accept it fully, frees us so we can freely love. My past pain has a lot to say about my purpose.

The past hurts have healed, my sadness is now joy, and my fears are now hope.

> "And we know that God causes everything to work together for the good of those who love God and are called according to his purpose for them."
>
> —Romans 8:28 (NLT)

THE STORMS FORM DUNES

Life is like a sand dune that forms with the wind, and new deposits make the dune stronger. We slowly form as we grow from a baby into adulthood. Storms come and go, but a sand dune is formed over time when native plants grow and root and stabilize the dune. Water may erode its foundation, but new growth always comes, providing strength and longevity. Just as the sand dune forms, a mother and father help form us, providing us with the stability to grow and be strong for the future.

We examine things that happen to us with different glasses or lenses. Reflecting on memories of my childhood and my mother's ability to hold us together as a family, I was able to see the positive side and strength she provided through the lens of acceptance and understanding rather than confusion and hurt. I spent many years trying to feel accepted and loved, so when we stopped talking (due to the boundaries I felt forced to form to protect myself), I continued to ask, "Why?"

It has been difficult for me not only to remember but to bring up good memories to memorialize with a stone of remembrance. I spent so much time focused on survival; that's all I knew. It was a long ten years with minimal to no contact with my mother. From 2010 to 2020, she wasn't speaking to me. That's a long ten years of asking myself, why? It was a very painful time. She passed away in 2020 after a battle with colon cancer (not COVID).

I will never know the answer to that "why." But I do know the answer to the other question: is it me? Or my fault that my mother refused to talk to me, or what did I do? I did nothing. No, it was not my fault. I also believe that no matter what age your child is, the human that you birthed out of your own flesh and blood, the *only* reason a mother would stop, give up on, or stop talking to that human is because of what we now talk more about—mental illness.

I chose to learn and grow as a person, a daughter, a wife, and a mother. Through my years, I've learned to depend on God because what else did I have more than my biological parents? I know who I am based on who God says I am, and I trust Him. Only God and Jesus can fill the hole after cleaning out the gunk from our humanness. I visualize myself opening my hands and giving my parents to God. He loves them more than I do or can.

I made peace with our relationship through lots of counseling sessions, and when she passed away without what some would say resolution or reconciliation, I was at peace.

Similar to having an infection or a disease, others in the family, my children, were affected over the years. The issue I had was how she treated Dennis and my children.

I find it very ironic that my mother, whom her entire life talked to me about our ancestors, decided not to meet her great-grandchildren.

Let that sink in.

She never met Rene's children, and honestly, that was her loss and decision.

THE DELTA

You cannot want something for people more than they want it for themselves. I wanted healthy relationships with my mother and family so badly. Did I try through the years? Yes! Did I finally resolve that I could not fix anything? Yes. My mother made her decision, and I can tell you that mental illness is real.

In looking at the past, though, what I want my children and grandchildren to know is that my mother (in her healthier years) did a lot of good for me growing up. Let me give you some examples.

She was the one who taught me to sew and put me in sewing classes in order that I could learn more. She put me in swimming lessons and took me to the beach. She put me in hula dance lessons. She took me to Girl Scouts and encouraged me in scouting. She had me take golf lessons, tennis lessons, and water skiing! Trying new things was encouraged. Taking risks was encouraged.

When I was thirteen, I asked her if I could join a "Walk for the Whales" fundraiser, like the walks we have today for causes. I was determined to participate, and I entered and walked around Diamond Head and areas all by myself! She allowed me to do this.

She drove me to my Lifesaving classes and picked me up late at night (nine p.m.) in the Aiea Heights area on Oahu.

She helped me get into Southern Illinois University and reach Southern Illinois with Aunt Mildred.

She went to college at the age of thirty-nine in Missoula, Montana, at Montana State University and got a BSN and RN degree. In fact, we graduated college just a few weeks apart! In May 1984, we went to each other's graduation. I was very proud of my mother for getting her nursing degree. This was also one of the few times that I felt she was proud of me. I believe she wanted more for me than she had. I think as women, each generation wants more for the next generation of women because we have had to fight for everything.

We both got on our feet after graduation, and she was able to fulfill her dream of moving back to Hawaii which she did in 1985. I think the divorce from my father hurt her immensely, although she never discussed it with me. I was happy for her when she met Leon, remarried, and appeared to be happy. It was short-lived, however, and that marriage lasted just over a year, resulting in another divorce. She wanted a new beginning, again, moving after living ten years in Hawaii back to the mainland.

This time, in 1995, my mom moved from Oahu to Atlanta to live near me. I was very happy to have my mother living close to me and our family. We finally would have family close by—something I missed out on as a kid. She bought a house just eight miles from us, and my children got to know her as their Granny. For the next ten years, until she moved to Pensacola, Florida, in 2006, I tried to be a "good daughter."

According to my mother, our relationship was based on a hierarchy, and I was expected to comply. She was the elder at the top of the family structure, and all information, questions, and decisions flowed down from her wisdom to us. This way of thinking was not mine nor Dennis' for our family.

After my mother moved close to us and we started having regular interactions it became obvious to us that this type of communication was exactly what she expected. Thus, the balancing act began. Keep my mother happy by listening and doing what she wanted us to do for our kids and her. Or push back. I didn't like to push back. That meant conflict, which I shy away from. Dennis did push back and probably was the only one that could do so. If you choose that path for a particular subject, you better be ready to counter it.

For example, when her father became ill and was likely not to live long, she wanted Rene, whom, by the way, they had never met and was nine at the time, to fly to Montana and meet him for the first time. Dennis thought this was inappropriate, especially for a child, to be able to handle the situation of meeting someone on their deathbed. He said no and was adamant that our daughter was not going. My mother was not happy that Dennis stood up and did not agree with her. She thought when she spoke, we better listen and do what she thought best. Why? She thought she was always right.

If I have learned anything in my twelve-step programs is that you do *not* tell other people what to do! Yes, she did have wisdom; she was the matriarch and wanted to be treated as an elder. Me and my family struggled with this because honestly, she wasn't very kind sometimes. Through regular counseling, I decided to set boundaries for myself and my family. This meant not always agreeing with her and she didn't like this. Our conversations got fewer and fewer. She didn't call and I stopped reaching out to protect myself.

She moved to Florida without even a goodbye. The following few years were very hard and often controlled my thoughts. I thought my life was defined by the "bad years." I believe she was mentally ill and didn't want or receive any treatment. What mother does not reach out or call when her daughter has breast cancer? Mine.

ANOTHER CURVE IN THE RIVER

In the middle of the "not speaking years," in 2015 to be exact, I was diagnosed with DCIS Stage zero ductile breast cancer. For years, I dealt with problems with one breast and previously had suspicious cells removed, watched, and scanned. The cancer was identified at an annual mammogram. Preventive things do work, and I am a testament to catching stuff early.

I decided to not only remove that breast but go ahead with a double mastectomy—the best decision for me because I don't have to worry anymore. I was hopeful that I would hear from my mother during this time of recovery. I did not. Yes, it did hurt. To this day I still deal with this emotion.

I know my mother did her best, and her childhood and life had many hurts, too. Her hurts were so many, yet she refused to get help.

The hurt, pain, and grief I have dealt with and resolved has been a journey, but my pain says a lot about my purpose. I want to have empathy and rise above my own pain and hurt to help others. I persevere so that I can produce fruit. I "do the work" to figure out how to share this pain and not hide.

Survival and denial were my best friends. I spent many years trying to "fix things." I'm a great problem solver, and

I can surely come up with an answer. I learned that I am not able to fix everything, nor do I need to try. Hiding and protecting myself shielded me from feeling the pain, abandonment, and yearning for a "normal" mother.

I can and I will do the hard things. Why? Because I broke the cycle of hurt people hurting people, at least in my immediate family.

THE UGLY TRUTH OF ADDICTION

You may or may not have heard that addiction runs in families.

It does. Both Dennis and I have alcohol abuse in our families.

The dreaded call. "Your brother died." My mom did call in November 2014 to tell me that my brother Charles had passed away unexpectedly and suddenly. He was only fifty-six years old. While not lingering with disease and suffering may be good, the sudden death of a sibling really gives a gut punch. We had to tell his son Matthew. We still had hopes that one day, my brother may get well enough to take care of Matt. Unfortunately, this hope was never realized.

I want you to know this rock of remembrance. My brother loved Jesus, and he loved his children. Addiction to alcohol does not discriminate who it chooses. Charles struggled, and his body gave out. While we will never truly know what caused his death, I do comprehend what damage years of not taking care of yourself will do. However, he called his children when he could. He tried to show he cared as best he could, and he never stopped loving them or his family.

When 2016 rolled around, addiction struck again in our family. Our son John had his entire colon removed in 2009 due to Crohn's disease/Ulcerative Colitis. Unfortunately, he got addicted to pain pills. It's not my complete story to tell;

it's his, but Dennis and I were affected and sought out recovery and coping for ourselves. Addiction is a family illness. Research shows that family members who struggle with addiction have more success recovering when they feel connected to family. We wanted to support John, for sure, but we also were dealing with our own denial, pain, stress, sleepless nights, regrets, and physical effects. I joined a local weekly Families Anonymous group, and we both went to Celebrate Recovery. Thankfully, God provided another major milestone for John of healing and sobriety. You always want the best for your children, and through recovery, we have learned how to support but not enable family members.

> "I have told you all this so that you may have peace in me. Here on earth, you will have many trials and sorrows. But take heart, because I have overcome the world."
>
> —John 16:33 (NLT)

LIVING WITH AN OPEN HEART

As I've shared, my husband Dennis and I met at college—one of the best things that ever happened to me. I rely on him a lot. I am a strong woman and believe that women can do most things men can, but Dennis has done so much for me.

We have been married for forty years! You heard it, forty! I cannot say enough good things about Dennis Champagne. Loyal, honest, consistent, and caring are just the first four adjectives that describe him.

In 2011, we both had *huge* health crises. He had untreated atrial fibrillation (A-Fib) for years, and his heart valve had weakened to the point where his heart wasn't pumping enough blood. He was weak and out of breath. The doctor told him he needed a valve repair and would need open heart surgery. We were scheduling this procedure when, out of the blue, I had a seizure while at work. I didn't know at the time it was a seizure, but after going to the ER, admittance to the hospital, and MRI, I was diagnosed with a benign meningioma. A slow-growing tumor of the lining of the brain that would either require daily medication (to prevent the seizures because it was putting pressure on my brain) or removal. Thankfully, the tumor was in a part of the brain that the doctor was positive he could remove 99 percent. I voted for removal, and three weeks later, I had brain surgery (remember the story of my friend visiting me at the hospital?). However, this meant that Dennis had to wait for his open-heart surgery. Less than six weeks after my surgery, Dennis had his surgery.

We both had positive outcomes and good prognosis for the future. His heart continues to be monitored, and he will probably take medication for the rest of his life for these heart issues. He has done what the doctor ordered and takes care of himself. He did have to have a med change a couple of times to get his heart back in rhythm.

In 2017, that ever-present rip current tried to pull me under again. Dennis was scheduled for a "routine" ablation to try and permanently fix the A-Fib, and before the doctor began the procedure, he had a reaction to the anesthesia. His heart "froze" and was pumping at 10 percent of what it was supposed to. They saved his life by inserting an Impella (a small pump that is inserted into one heart ventricle and pumps blood to the aorta), and lots of prayers were lifted to God. I may have prayed, "Please, Lord, please spare his life, and I will" —I can't remember, but God did save him.

I went on to spend the next few years with PTSD because I kept thinking I would lose him.

Dennis tells me, "I am going to die. We all will. Just not now." He's right, though. God holds our lives so gently in His hands. He made our bodies strong and resilient but also so vulnerable.

I am writing all this to let you know that, yes, we will have troubles in this world, but we also have the peace that only the Lord can give us. I held on to this peace through our health troubles that, thankfully, we both overcame. We are dealing with the consequences, but as Dennis says, it's better than the alternative.

We talk to our children about life after we are gone. We talk about death and life when we go to be with Jesus. While I do not like thinking about it, I have concluded that, yes, I probably rely on Dennis too much. God gave him to me, and I have learned so much. Living with open hearts means living each day to the fullest, meeting people where they are, and always being on the lookout for where the Holy Spirit will guide us next.

The tides come in and out and help shape the sand. I am forever grateful for Dennis in my life and thank God daily. I place a rock here.

> "When I am afraid,
> I put my trust in you.
> In God, whose word I praise,
> in God I trust; I shall not be afraid.
> What can flesh do to me?"
>
> —Psalm 56:3-4 (ESV)

"Shout with joy to the Lord, all the earth!
Worship the Lord with gladness.
Come before him, singing with joy.
Acknowledge that the Lord is God!
He made us, and we are his.
We are his people, the sheep of his pasture.
Enter his gates with thanksgiving;
go into his courts with praise.
Give thanks to him and praise his name.
For the Lord is good.
His unfailing love continues forever,
and his faithfulness continues to each generation."

—Psalm 100 (NLT)

FREEDOM FROM THE RIP TIDE

Every time I chose to persevere, each choice I made to move forward has built and healed me from the inside out.

I'm living in the freedom and hard-earned joy I fought for when it would have been easier to give up.

I tell myself, "Don't look back to the past." He is doing something new; look forward.

> [18] "But forget all that—it is nothing compared to what I am going to do.
> [19] For I am about to do something new. See, I have already begun! Do you not see it? I will make a pathway through the wilderness. I will create rivers in the dry wasteland."
> —Isaiah 43:18-19 (NLT)

Thankfully, God continues to build on the foundation of the healing I have already done. Sometimes, or if I am honest, most times, I don't see the good that comes out of the last season, but it's there, and it's necessary. I am not the same person I was when I began this writing journey.

I trust and believe that God's ways are higher than mine.

I will stay the course and trust that I am not off track. I trust that nothing can stop the good work God is committed to doing in my life, and I open my heart fully and embrace what has and is to come.

Remember my military moving around days, which I described earlier? Here is a big stone of remembrance I want to share.

My children grew up in the house Dennis and I still live in, and my daughter lives in the next neighborhood over. Literally, I can walk there, and it's just a two-minute drive in the same neighborhood where they crossed the creek years ago to go to their friend's house.

My two older grandchildren attend the same elementary school that their mom went to. The younger two grandchildren are only a three-hour drive away outside of Nashville.

These Grands are the joy of my heart. My why! Dennis and I enjoy every minute we spend playing cards and games, crawling on the floor with trucks, going to museums and national parks, driving them to appointments, or taekwondo. We embrace all of it.

I pinch myself almost daily. Is this real life? Yes. God is faithful and kind.

My children know without a shadow of a doubt they are loved by their mother and father. We tell them every time we talk. They are adults with their own families, and while I'm sure, as parents, we could have done some things differently, my goal to resolve my brokenness so that they can be more whole is achieved.

It is imperative to let go of the past so that your hands can be empty to receive what God has for you in the future.

I have been faithful, and a faithful God will not let

anything in my life go to waste. He will use it all in ways I can't yet fully see.

Better things are yet to come.

There are numerous wounds in our hearts throughout the generations, but God calls each of us on our journeys to tell or pass on the remembrances—the good and the bad.

> [7] "He is so rich in kindness and grace that he purchased our freedom with the blood of his Son and forgave our sins. [8] He has showered his kindness on us, along with all wisdom and understanding."
>
> —Ephesians 1:7-8 (NLT)

A LETTER TO MY HEAVENLY FATHER

Dear Heavenly Father,
You were with me in the storms.

It's sometimes easier to look in the rear-view mirror and see all the places where you were with me. Like footprints in the sand.

On the plane flying from Guam to Montana. You were with me.

Arriving in the snow in Carbondale to attend Southern Illinois University, not knowing a soul.

You were with me.

Through my and Dennis's health trials. You were with me.

I am thankful that you never left me even though I often struggle to find my own way.

I praise you in the storms and in the peace. Thank you for calling me your daughter and giving me the "stones of remembrances" I can share to bring your glory.

You are mightier than the waves of the sea!

You are a God of grace, love kindness and gentleness. But the ocean is a picture of your power! The ocean is so big, so mighty, just an earthly glimpse of you! Thank you for this picture.

Thank you for calming the storms and waves of my life. May I seek you always. Amen!

Your Daughter, Walking with the King!
Alice

A LETTER TO MY EARTHLY FATHER

I wanted to make a trip to Guam to see where I lived in 1978, where I graduated high school and worked. I reached out to ask if my father would be open to a visit. I was told, "No. Do not come."

How did this make me feel? Sad, but most of all, sad for my earthly father. He does not choose to know me, and that is his loss.

So, Dad, this is what I wanted to say to you:

Dad, I forgive you. You are free.

Long ago, I gave up the right to hurt you back for hurting me. That's what forgiveness is.

I hold on to no hurt feelings.

I can't live with brokenness in my heart from how I grew up. God has pieced me back together.

I have too many good things that God has given me.

You are free. I hope you will accept that you are free.

Free to love God and be loved. Free from condemnation.

I would have liked to tell you this face to face, but it was your choice for me not to go to Guam so we could see each other.

That's okay. I am God's child, and I am loved by my Heavenly Father.

I am God's workmanship, and I have been adopted as God's child.

I pray that you can breathe in God's refreshing grace and know you are loved by Him.

I cannot get back the years that separated us as a family, but I am at peace and hope that you can find your own peace, too.

Your daughter,
Alice

NAVIGATING THE WATERS OF LIFE

Our parents do the best they can with what they were given to raise us. I'm not throwing my parents under the bus because we are all imperfect. I attempted to do better than the last generation, and hopefully, you will succeed as well.

As adults, we are all responsible for overcoming any negative consequences we have been faced with by imperfect parents.

It's not easy, but I encourage you not to give up.

Keep seeking.

Keep praying.

> "Rejoice in our confident hope. Be patient in trouble and keep on praying."
>
> —Romans 12:12 (NLT)

Through study, seeking truth in what God says, prayer, and community (you are not alone), I pray you continue to take steps to freedom from anxiety, depression, past hurts, and anything else that is holding you back from the person God created you to be.

This is what I am referring to when I titled this book *Better Things Are Yet to Come*—when you choose to move forward—despite everything you have experienced in life, know that God will never give up on you. He wants better things for you.

He will make rivers out of dry wastelands. He parted the river in order that His people could cross safely. What are the things that are waiting for you to do at this time of your life?

Let's keep going—lovingly, kindly, courageously, genuinely, compassionately, selflessly, hospitably, and passionately—to build more stones of remembrance for God to show His Glory through us.

ACKNOWLEDGMENTS AND THE NEXT THING TO COME

What is the best way to thank God for all He has done to keep me close, love me, and care for me over the years? God adopted me into His family when I was young, guided me through all the relocating, kept me safe in the turbulent years of high school and college, and helped me graduate with a BS in Engineering that I was not the slightest bit prepared for. He led me to meet and marry my husband, who is generous, kind, and loving, and steered me through an amazing career path, working in various jobs I was passionate about. God gave me two amazing children who never cease to teach me more, navigated helping my nieces and nephews like my own children, and was faithful and made me a Nana.

If this is not enough, He continues to teach me new things and give me confidence to fulfill new opportunities for Him to use me to help others. During the writing of this book, a business I was a brand advocate for closed, providing me with a new path to choose. He opened a door for me to be a Certified Christian Life Coach, assisting others by facilitating personal growth and change through action. I have been "coaching" unofficially for years, just without a certification or title. While writing this book I realized that God has prepared me fully for this next phase or season in my journey. I'm saying yes to this new purpose and am excited to discover the fruit of such a time as this.

There is a time for everything:

> "For everything there is a season,
> a time for every activity under heaven.
> A time to be born and a time to die.
> A time to plant and a time to harvest.
> A time to kill and a time to heal.
> A time to tear down and a time to build up.
> A time to cry and a time to laugh.
> A time to grieve and a time to dance.
> A time to scatter stones and a time to gather stones.
> A time to embrace and a time to turn away.
> A time to search and a time to quit searching.
> A time to keep and a time to throw away.
> A time to tear and a time to mend.
> A time to be quiet and a time to speak.
> A time to love and a time to hate.
> A time for war and a time for peace."
>
> —Ecclesiastes 3: 1-8 (NLT)

We all need our tribe to love and support us, and I thank you for encouraging and walking with me as I faced the pain and healing process to reach this point so that I could write this book.

Thank you to my husband, Dennis, my children, Rene and John, my extended family and friends—I wish I had adequate words to tell you how important you are to me, and I appreciate you being there for me through all the good and hard things. I love you beyond measure.

I also want to thank my editor, Rachel Arterberry, at Making A Way Writing Services and my photographer, Masha Champagne.

Last, but not least, thank you for reading my memoir. I pray that my life stones of remembrance help you in your life, and to God be the Glory.

And finally, when my grandchildren and their grandchildren ask, "Nana, what are the stones of remembrance?" I will explain what God did for Joshua when He parted the sea for all to safely cross the river and remind them that God is always fighting for them. I will encourage them to reflect on their lives and mark their remembrances (with a stone) to memorialize all God has done. He is faithful throughout all generations.

> [20] "Now all glory to God, who is able, through his mighty power at work within us, to accomplish infinitely more than we might ask or think. [21] Glory to him in the church and in Christ Jesus through all generations forever and ever! Amen."
>
> —Ephesians 3:20-21 (NLT)

Gratefully,
Alice Jeanne Martratt Champagne
August 2024

www.alice-champagne.com

www.ingramcontent.com/pod-product-compliance
Lightning Source LLC
Chambersburg PA
CBHW050225100526
44585CB00017BA/2010